the PARENT TRIP

the
PARENT TRIp

*From High Heels and Parties
to Highchairs and Potties*

Jenna McCarthy

Bella Luna Press
P.O. Box 30624
Santa Barbara, CA 93130
www.bellalunapress.com

Cover and interior design by Chris Hall/Ampersand
Author photo copyright © 2008 by Renée Vernon

Library of Congress Control Number: 2007941136

ISBN-13 978-0-9799135-6-3

Printed in Canada on 100% recycled paper

for dad

Contents

Acknowledgments — ix

Disclaimer — xiii

Prologue — xv

1. Anyone Seen My Maternal Instincts? — 1

2. How Babies Are Really Made — 7
   Trip Tip—Why It's Better to Be You Than Gwen Stefani — 12

3. He Shoots, He Scores! — 17
   Trip Tip—Not Every Burp Belongs in the Baby Book — 22

4. The Rehearsal Dinner—or the Entire Wedding? — 27
   Trip Tip—Take My Husband...Please! — 35

5. 287 Days Is a Really, Really Long Time — 41
   Trip Tip—Baby Registries Are for the Greedy
   (and Other Dumb Thoughts You Might One Day Regret) — 47

6. This Just In: They Don't Call It *Labor* For Nothing — 51
   Trip Tip—Call It What You Will — 56

7. I've Gotta Get Out of This Place — 61
   Trip Tip—Is the Energizer Bunny the Devil in Disguise? — 66

8. So *That's* What They're For! — 71

9. Pay at the Pump — 77
   Trip Tip—Midnight in the Garden of...Pure Evil — 81

10. Can I Get Some Help Around Here?   85
    Trip Tip—Hiring a Hand to Rock the Cradle   90

11. Your Baby Is Cute, Too—but Can She Spell "Pretentious"?   95

12. You Want to Have *What?*   101
    Trip Tip—"Take Me Now, Big Guy!" and
    Other Things You Won't Be Saying Anytime Soon   105

13. We Need a Bigger House to Hold All of This Crap   111

14. Parents Say (and Do) the Darnedest Things   115
    Trip Tip—Mommy's Dead:
    Fun and Enlightening Tales for Tots   120

15. Sleep in Heavenly Peace *(Please!)*   123

16. Why My Pediatrician Has a Summer House and I Don't   129
    Trip Tip—Is My Baby Okay?
    (A Field Guide to Overreacting)   134

17. I've Been to Hell—and It Looks Suspiciously Like My Kitchen   139
    Trip Tip—Chew on This: A Helpful, Handy Baby-Feeding Primer   145

18. Time Isn't the Only Thing That's Crawling   149
    Trip Tip—The "Five Second Rule" and Other
    Disgusting Parenting Practices You Will Embrace   154

19. Load Up the Wagon—We're Hitting the Road   159
    Trip Tip: Oh, the Places You'll Go:
    What You Should Know Before Traveling with Baby   164

20. School Daze: Did I Miss the Memo?   171

21. The Definition of Insanity   177

    Epilogue   181

Acknowledgments

I was an expert on parenting until I had kids. Similarly, before embarking on *The Parent Trip* (the manuscript part, at least), I "knew" what it took to produce a book: You sat down, you wrote and when you got to the end, you had a neat, fat, magically bound stack of pages. Of course, you did this alone. I mean, how many hands can fit on a keyboard anyway?

Now I know better. Turns out that if you want likable kids and a decent book, it really does take a village (plus a few great babysitters and lots of charitable family members and friends). To wit, I am eternally grateful for the support, advice and camaraderie generously offered to me by the following people:

Deep and heartfelt thanks to my dad, Douglas McCarthy, for your boundless love, your wicked humor and for insisting that I never, ever work for anyone but myself. I miss you every day. Thanks to Laurie Powers for eagerly reading every word I write, even if many of them make you cringe. To my mom, Maria McCarthy, for instilling in me a love of books with ten thousand selfless trips to the Ormond Beach Library. Brian McCarthy, you keep me in stitches. I owe a massive debt of gratitude to 24/7 Construction (aka Captain Jack and Linda McCa-

for your incomparable support, unconditional love and kick-ass plumbing skills. To Heidi McCarthy for encouraging me enough for two. My dear friend Pamela Gillett: Your laid-back attitude and deliciously bad influence make life fun. Kim Vela, your friendship is a gift I treasure daily. Kirsten Kemp Becker, what did I do before I met you? Whatever it was, I hope I never have to do it again. To the talented Starshine Roshell, you continually raise the bar and keep me on my toes. Tami Sherman—would that all of my friends and fans were as fiercely loyal as you are. Teresa Polito, thanks for always giving and never keeping score (I'm pretty sure I owe you). Cheryl Richardson, I want to be you— but knowing you is a spectacular consolation prize. Jennifer Williams and Jodi R.R. Smith, you believed in me from the get-go. Sally Franz, you dazzle with your energy, passion, grasp of daunting technology and way with words. Jennifer Fleece, you are wise and wonderful, and I am lucky to have you in my life. To my faithful friends, readers and real-mom inspirations Shelly Caserta, Darrell Casoria, Lynn Long, L. Michelle Todd, Courtney Adams, Vicki Moss, Kristin Michler, Jenifer Paredes, Mariaelena Welch, Janis Byars, Courtney Peralta, Kim Tank, Margo Ochoa, Laurel O'Connor, Barbara McWhirter: If I lifted a glass for each time you made me laugh until I cried, I'd be in detox for seven years. Special thanks to my fun and fabulous pals Susie Pollard, Shemai Rodriguez, Michele Putman and Tanya Winch for loving me enough to overlook otherwise irrelevant content and tell me I'm great. Yvonne Duran, your input is invaluable. Judy Pfleger, you are a creative genius with energy and ideas to spare. To Nancy "Goddess" Gottesman, for always talking (and cracking) me up. Adam Vela: Author warrants that to the best of Author's knowledge you are a flipping legal genius, nice guy and all-around rock star. Guru Jerry Jenkins, I am your grasshopper for life. MaryEllen Mathieu, your heart, talent and enthusiasm are as big as the Pacific. The folks at KTYD, thanks for giving me a job even though we all know I'm utterly unemployable. Kathy Nenneker, you are a one-woman editorial dream team; it is a privilege to work with you. Cathryn Michon, you redefine genius. To Coco Waddell and Tamara Monosoff for spilling your secrets; Ann Douglas for the inside scoop; Paula Page for your infectious energy and can-do spirit; Michael Gerrish for a decade of long-distance support (and for marrying the sweetest and most bighearted lady on the planet). Kelly and Paul Brooks—your generosity and goodness are humbling. I have a massive and possibly unhealthy appreciation for the time and efforts of Lara Runnels and John J. Strauss; your kindness will not be forgotten. Ginormous thankfulness to Janet Evanovich for selflessly lending me your ear and a helluva plug. Chris Hall, Ron Larson and Renée Vernon: Your collective creative brilliance makes me look good. Bottomless affection for Sarah "Yaya" Hooper, Aaren Alpert, Olga Chakarayan and Amanda Hess for being part of our family in every sense of the word. Sharon Cohen, you planted the seed. Peg Moline, you made it all possible. Paul Reiser and Dave Barry—thanks for the glowing endorsements that obviously got lost in the mail. You guys rock!

Sadie Allison, you gave me the courage to take the plunge and the skills to do it gracefully. If I live to be 110, I can never repay you.

Most importantly, to the beautiful, magnificent Sophie Bella and Sasha Laurel for the incredible gift that is this journey. Without you my life would be aimless and hollow, even though I'd probably wear better shoes.

And finally, I owe my strength and sanity to Joe Coito, my co-captain, conscience and best friend, for inspiring, amusing and enduring me every single day. It is an honor to be your wife, and there is no one with whom I'd rather share this ride. Not even Gabriel Byrne if he were younger and taller. I swear.

P.S. Oh yeah, and to every guy who ever dumped me, every surly retail clerk who ever snubbed me and every catty, upwardly mobile coworker who thoughtlessly dug the pointy heel of her Jimmy Choo into my back trying to get ahead: Thank you from the bottom of my happy, forgiving heart. The rage and disappointment you fueled made me work harder than I ever thought possible. This book's for you!

P.P.S. If you invested a good ten minutes in this section only to find that I forgot your name, please forgive me. It's been a stressful year, and I couldn't have done it without your support. I'm just glad our relationship is so rock-solid that we can get past this little oversight.

Disclaimer

The purpose of this book is to entertain. Some readers may even find it informative. But in no way is it intended to instruct or educate. There may very well be mistakes, sweeping generalizations or gross exaggerations in content, and if it were 100 percent grammatically correct, the author would, quite frankly, be shocked. Furthermore, the author willingly concedes that many of the events and methodologies depicted in this book may not represent the pinnacle of parenting, and urges the reader to use his or her judgment before following suit. Finally, this book definitely is not intended to be a substitute for professional medical advice. Women who are having a difficult time conceiving should see a fertility specialist; pregnant woman are urged to seek qualified, routine prenatal care; and if your six-month-old gets a worm stuck in his nose, please take him to his pediatrician (promptly).

....

Prologue

[*Interior: Brady-style home, Florida, 1978. Nine-year-old* JENNA *runs around the kitchen island, through the adjacent dining room and back into the kitchen.* JENNA'S MOM *chases* JENNA *with one slipper on her foot and the other slipper in her hand. As they circle the island several times on opposite sides,* JENNA'S MOM *swats unsuccessfully at* JENNA *across the island with the slipper in her hand. After several circles* JENNA *escapes up the stairs to her room, where she slams the door with a thundering thwack.*]

JENNA [*behind door*] I hate you, I hate you, I hate you, I HATE you!
JENNA'S MOM [*shouting, ominously, voice shaking*] One day you're going
　　to have a daughter *just like you!*

_____

[*Interior: ugly high school cafeteria, Florida, 1985. Sixteen-year-olds* JENNA *and* KRISTIN *sit pressing stacks of paper towels onto slices of soggy, undercooked pizza. (How they can even hold their heads up is a mystery, seeing as each sports at least ten pounds of hairspray and earrings the size of baseballs. Well, it is 1985.) Both make disgusted faces.*]

KRISTIN You doing anything this weekend?
JENNA Nope. You?

KRISTIN Yeah, my family is going up to St. Augustine. I was supposed to babysit for the Trevinos. You want to do it?

JENNA Nope.

KRISTIN Please?

JENNA No way.

KRISTIN Come on! The kids are ADORABLE!

JENNA No kids are adorable. They're all dirty and loud and they smell ·like sweat. [*shudders on the last word*]

KRISTIN They pay five bucks an hour.

JENNA I don't give a crap. Never. No. Ugh.

KRISTIN [*exasperated*] Fine, I'll ask Karan.

[*Interior: dimly lit, romantic restaurant, California, 1997.* JENNA *and* JOE *(both thirtyish) hold hands across a small table. They gaze intently into each other's eyes. The restaurant is empty except for the couple, obviously on a first date. A waiter shuffles by and clears his throat, trying to get their attention. It is late and he wants to go home.* JENNA *and* JOE *remain oblivious.*]

JOE So, how do you feel about kids?

JENNA You mean children? [*laughs nervously*] Oh, I LOVE them! Always have. My sister has a baby. It breaks my heart that they live in North Carolina. It's so far away! [*shakes head wistfully*]

JOE Wow. I feel the exact same way. I have three older sisters and I just can't get enough of my nieces and nephews. Seriously, I can't wait to have kids of my own. That's what life is all about, don't you think?

[JENNA *nods, swallows visibly, smiles weakly. Camera pans in to show one hand nervously twisting her napkin in her lap. After all,* JENNA *really likes this guy—but this may be going a little too far.*]

....

Anyone Seen My Maternal Instincts?

I was twelve the first time I had the dream. Maybe the health class I was taking at the time put the idea in my head; perhaps it was the litter of kittens our family cat had recently delivered. It certainly wasn't because I was worried about getting knocked up. That would be at least another four and a half years.

I have the dream many more times over the next two decades, although unlike some recurring dreams this one is always exactly the same: I'm naked in an elevator that appears to be stuck. I am alone, which (being naked and all) may seem to be a good thing, but it's actually a bad thing because I am pregnant. And in that way you just "know" things in dreams, I know that I must hold both of my hands underneath my titanic belly; if I don't, the baby will rip through my skin and plop onto the floor. Whether I'm worried about my health, the baby's health, the sanitation conditions in the elevator or the fact that *I am not ready to have a baby and this one therefore must stay on the inside of my body* is unclear. All I know is that I cannot let go, which means I cannot press the panic button or do anything else to improve my unfortunate situation.

In this dream I am surprisingly calm and I never try to scream for help. (Aren't dreams crazy? I mean, you're seeing this thing and it's like a movie but it's *you* and it's utterly real. And it's not like your best friend is there to shout "Hey, idiot! Why don't you try yelling your fool head off?") Instead, I wait. My arms ache from the enormous strain. Time crawls to a halt. Minutes become days. I stand and I cup my massive middle and eventually I wake up.

I'd have other pregnancy dreams from time to time—in one particularly memorable one, I go through the hellish ordeal of labor and delivery, only to be handed a well-swaddled raccoon. These hallucinations clearly proved one thing: This breeding business was not for me.

There were other signs, too. Although I adored baby dolls and Barbies, my childhood yearnings to nurture stopped there. Unlike the other girls my age, I never ached to play that ultimate make-believe game known as babysitting. Puke and poop and Play-Doh and temper tantrums and hours of inane cartoon-watching on a strange sofa? No thanks. The awesome responsibility implied in the job—you had to keep your charges not only happy and dry, but *alive,* for crying out loud—wasn't daunting to me in the least. It just didn't sound like fun. Not even the lure of junk food (all my babysitting friends swore they ate a nonstop stockpile of crap on the job) could change my mind.

Soon enough I actually *was* having sex and the pregnancy threat became real. I went on the pill long before the maiden voyage and when the act finally was consummated, I made my boyfriend use a condom on top of it (so to speak), just to be safe. AIDS wasn't a threat back then and STDs were only a concern for the slutty girls who smoked cigarettes in the bathroom. The singular impetus for employing that revoltingly slimy sheath was to bolster my efforts to prevent an extremely unwanted pregnancy. Period.

I saw comedian Jerry Seinfeld do a bit on stage once about scuba diving. The funnyman was questioning the sanity of a sport whose primary goal is survival. "There's a fish, there's a turtle, there's some coral, there's an eel, don't die, don't die..." he'd chant, and the audience was in stitches. Well, that was sex for me. "That feels good, oh yeah, right there, that's nice, don't get pregnant, don't get pregnant...." Mercifully, I didn't.

When my friends—including my very own sister—began procreating, I'd say and do all of the things I knew were required of me: I threw baby showers, oohed and aahed over miniature shoes and handkerchief-size blankets, played pregnancy word scramble and the poopy diaper game with dozens of tea-sipping, mini-quiche-and-cucumber-sandwich-eating women I didn't know. Occasionally I even tried to win. But I never envied any of my swollen sisters, and if I'm being totally honest here—and believe me, I am—it was a chore to remember to fawn appropriately once the actual babies arrived.

After all, when someone you love has a baby and you don't, and you aren't planning to anytime soon and still think happy hour is the best reason to get out of bed in the afternoon, I think it's natural to be a little torn.

On the surface I was always all smiles and support. "Wow!" I'd gush, instinctively reaching out to lay my hand on the still-flat belly in question. Now that there was a fetus in the room, my gut response— "Holy shit!"—didn't seem appropriate. "There's a human life in there!" I might add stupidly. "Isn't that just the most magical and beautiful thing in the world?"

But the very large imaginary thought bubble over my head would read more like this: *"What in God's name are you thinking?* You're going to be chained to that child for the rest of your life, or at least the rest of hers. (Until I know otherwise, I always assume it's a girl. All women secretly want girls, although we can't admit it because we never know what we're going to get and we don't want to look picky or we might get something horrible, just to teach us a lesson.) So you're going to have this daughter, at least until she grows up and realizes mothers are embarrassing at best and complete failures at worst, and publicly renounces you and your relationship in *People* magazine, which she'll be able to do because everyone knows screwed-up moms always have famous kids. Just when you think your life can't get any worse, she will go on to pen *The New York Times* bestseller *Living With the Worst Mom on the Planet: A Daughter's True Tale.* But long before that, she is going to want piano, soccer, tuba, scuba, ballet and hockey lessons, not to mention pierced ears and a puppy of her very own, and right then and there you can kiss your annual spa weekend goodbye. And your weekly manicures, which you won't need anymore because who's going to see you? It's not like you'll be getting out of the house. Of course, ragged nails are going to be the least of your worries with the stretch marks, *National Geographic* boobs and wardrobe of sweatpants waiting for you as the New Mom Club's newest member. Maybe in fifteen or twenty years you'll wear nice clothes again, but until then, chances are you won't be able to afford them or you won't be able to fit into them. And even if you can and you are, you'll never be able to get the pureed carrot-and-spinach medley out of them. Social life? You won't have one. Sex life? Ha. Your days are going to be a sad blur of homework and heartbreak and broken bones and lice. (Have you ever combed a head for lice? For the record, it's disgusting.) You will embarrass her just by existing. You will do and say every single thing you swore on stacks of Bibles that you wouldn't, like 'Because I said so' and 'Don't talk to me with that tone of voice!' (The only reason you won't use the ever-popular 'Just wait until your father comes home!' is because her father stopped coming home a long time ago.) Your darling daughter, the one you played Beethoven to in the womb and fed at your very breast, will snarl and hiss and lie to you and tell you to your face that she hates you. One day you will take Precious shopping for school clothes, and when you won't buy her the $98 jeans she wants, she will throw a temper tantrum right in the middle of Bloomingdale's and you will have to drag her out of the store screaming, 'You can go to school in your stinking pajamas for all I care!' and it won't be until you get home that you realize she has lost both of her brand-new sandals, one of which you vaguely recall seeing under a sale rack, now that you think about it, and the other of which could be just about anywhere. She will drink beer when she is thirteen. She will smoke pot when she is fourteen. She will have sex when she is fifteen, but possibly even sooner because you had sex when you were fifteen and you weren't even popular, but she will be because she will have had a lifetime of Internet access and on-demand TV. She'll need braces. She'll need bras—at least you hope she'll need bras because, in all truth, you really didn't, although you insisted on having them anyway. She'll want ski trips, her own car, designer everything and probably either a nose job or a tattoo or both. And what if she turns out to be a lesbian? What if she becomes a trash collector or a lawyer or one of those women who marry a millionaire on national TV and then pose in *Penthouse*? What if she looks like your Uncle Fred?"

Alas, I never uttered a word of this—and it's a good thing I didn't. Because before long *I* was the one having my midsection measured in squares of toilet paper, and honestly there's nothing worse than a festive chorus of "I told you so." Except maybe the first bowel movement after you give birth.

2

....

How Babies Are Really Made

Obviously there's a huge gray area between the black and white extremes of "Never gonna do it" and "Do you think we should paint the nursery bisque or buttercream?" For many, the shift might start with a vague observation, something along the lines of "Wow, lots of people have *babies*. Not for me—but interesting." Then perhaps your ob-gyn casually remarks that if you ever want to have a family, you'd better (not her words) "shit or get off the pot." This could lead to several heated "I-don't-know-maybe-soon-but-not-now-but-if-not-now-then-*when?*" debates with one's partner. Eventually, by simply entertaining the idea of reproducing, it gets accepted into your subconscious as a likely, if not probable, event. (This is a gradual process, sort of like when people insist on tossing around words like "celebutante" and "yogalates," and finally poor Merriam-Webster has no choice but to stick them in the dictionary.) The next thing you know, you announce to the world that you're "trying" and there's no going back.

Have you ever sat down to eat a nice slice of French toast and found Celine Dion's smiling face staring back at you from your plate?

Me neither, but that would be less shocking to me than the sudden and overwhelming urge I have to reproduce.

Here's how it goes down: I am thirty-two, married and have just arrived at my gynecologist's office for my annual exam. There are six other women in the waiting room, and every last one of them appears to be attempting to smuggle something large and round into the exam room under her top. Every smuggler has at least one hand casually resting on her protruding abdomen, and all of them wear self-satisfied grins. A feeling sweeps over me, and for a split-second I actually feel nauseous. Can it be...is this actually...am I really...*jealous?* But it can be—it must be—because I am! I want to be one of them! I want a baby. How long has this been going on? And why didn't anyone tell me? *I* want a baby. I *want* a baby. I want a *baby.* It's unbelievable. I made this appointment today to discuss having an IUD put in. Even an hour ago, I'd have sworn I didn't even *have* a biological clock, and suddenly the thing is ticking like Big freaking Ben.

"I'm thinking about getting pregnant," I tell the nurse who leads me into the exam room. Sure, I should probably discuss the idea with my husband, but it's not like I'm scheduling a date with a turkey baster or secretly flushing my birth control pills down the toilet here. I'm just throwing out a hypothetical idea. Still, I feel dizzy just saying the words out loud.

"Okay, I'll let the doctor know," she remarks, making a note on my chart and disappearing from the room. *Hello? Did you not hear what I just said? I am considering creating a human life, right here in my body! One with arms, legs, ears, the whole bit.* I'm not expecting an award—I realize this has been done before—but a little enthusiasm might be nice.

"Let's have a baby!" I announce that evening, throwing my arms around my husband's neck by way of a greeting. Joe has wanted kids since *he* was a kid. The one thing I am certain of is that I will not have to talk him into this.

"What?" he asks suspiciously.

My eyes widen into disks.

"I said, 'Let's have a baby!'" I repeat, breathless from excitement.

"Why?" he demands.

Why have a baby? Okay, it's a legitimate question, I suppose, but certainly not the response I was expecting.

"Because we can!" I shout. "Because we have the best dog on the planet! Because we are mature and responsible and have decent jobs and a spare bedroom and we'll be awesome parents! Wait a minute, why am I having to convince you that we should have a baby? I thought you *wanted* kids! I thought you'd be beside yourself!" I'm starting to get a little ticked off here.

"I do!" he shouts back. "I am! I want kids more than anything in the world. You know that. I'm just surprised that you made a sudden and complete turnaround, and I think it's fair to ask why."

I can't tell him about the smugglers and the jealousy and the nausea. I just can't. He won't understand.

"I changed my mind," the petulant brat I have become in the past four minutes spits back.

"You're serious?" he asks cautiously.

"As a heart attack," I declare.

"And you won't change your mind?" he demands.

"I won't change my mind," I hrumph.

"Promise?" he insists.

"I want this as much as you do, honey," I say. Implausibly, I do.

Some people might tell you that trying-to-make-a-baby sex is the best possible kind, fostering intimacy and togetherness in a way no other activity can. These people are insane. Well, maybe the first two or three times you go at it with no protection whatsoever, there's a bit of an aren't-we-naughty thrill and maybe a fleeting sensation of heightened closeness. This is almost automatically followed by what's scientifically referred to as the "oh crap!" panic moment. After all, you've spent years—possibly decades—and untold sums of money on condoms, pills, gels, sponges, patches, caps, rings and injections, doing everything in your power not to get knocked up. You've wondered and worried about that scary 2–22 percent failure rate of your preferred method, and possibly even waged the "abortion or adoption" debate in your head—even if neither of these is, in fact, a viable option for a myriad of moral, ethical or personal reasons. You not only know that RU-486 was *not a Star Wars* character, but you may even have an expired prescription for it hidden in a dusty shoebox stuffed way under your bed. Now suddenly, here you are making an emotional hairpin turn and actively attempting to conceive. If that's not enough to mess with your head, I don't know what is. Even if you've decided that you are absolutely, 100 percent ready to have a baby, there is a very wise, very evolved part of your brain that knows that no one who has never had a baby is ever really ready to have a baby. How can you be?

While procreative sex doesn't exactly feel like a *chore,* it definitely feels…purposeful. First there's this: The entire time we're doing the deed, *I'm thinking about my internal organs.* I can picture that damned diagram that's featured in every woman's health book or article, the "female anatomy" illustration that vaguely resembles a ram's head. There's the urethra, there's the cervix, there are the fallopian tubes. Wonder where the little ovum is right now. What's she doing? Does she have any idea she is about to be attacked by a mob of eager sperm? I actually feel kind of bad for her. If you have never thought about how seriously weird the reproduction process is, I urge you not to start *while you are having sex and trying to make a baby.* It isn't exactly the stuff of erotica. I am not in bed with my handsome husband, I am in tenth-grade biology class learning about mitosis, meiosis, fragmentation, cross-pollination and suckering and thinking to myself: *Who came up with this crazy system we've got here, anyhow?*

And then there's the aftermath. Where once we might have engaged in a cozy spooning session before drifting off to sleep, now Joe flips me onto my back, thrusts a pillow under my rear end and grabs my ankles, hauling them high into the air. "Gotta help the guys reach the finish line!" he practically shouts. (Incidentally, he never, *ever,* refers to his sperm as "gals." Not once. But that egg? Oh, she's mine and she's a girl, damn it.)

Romantic, huh?

I once wrote a magazine article on infertility, and after doing the research I thought it was downright shocking that anyone *ever* gets pregnant. The lone successful sperm has the best chance of reaching and impregnating an egg (presuming you are producing viable eggs, and who really knows until you have this checked?) in the two days before ovulation and on the day of ovulation. The day *after* ovulation, even the strongest swimmer's fighting chances decline to a discouraging zero percent. Yup, miss that golden window by one lousy day and you're looking at a minimum of four more weeks of torturous waiting. Of course, most women have only the vaguest idea when they are ovulating, which is why there are over-the-counter tests and complicated "fertility awareness" protocols that aspiring parents often employ.

We start charting my "basal body temperature," because a slight rise generally corresponds with the release of the precious egg. But you have to have a baseline for comparison in order to recognize your personal spike, so this is not a fleeting endeavor. I become intimately familiar with my bodily secretions (when trying to conceive, you want a sticky "egg white" consistency to your, ahem, cervical mucus, not the otherwise murky, watery goop), a phenomenon I was happy to completely ignore up until this point. I try to pay painfully close attention to my abdominal sensations ("Was that a twinge? I think I felt a twinge!") because I am not one of those women—and I have heard they exist—who instinctively knows when she ovulates. I feel guilty saying this, but until recently I'd never given my dear, darling eggs a passing thought.

We have lots of sex in the morning, even though I vastly prefer to make love with fresh breath, because some not-so-great studies indicate there may be an infinitesimal increase in sperm count in the pre-dawn hours. Foreplay goes from "I can't wait to get naked with you" to "Hurry! Get in here! My BBT is 99.8!"

For our entire lives, we have been a pair of lust-driven hedonists, doing what feels good, when it feels good, in self-centered pursuit of personal pleasure. But within days of deciding to carve our own personal notch into the world overpopulation belt, already we've assumed the parental frame of mind. This isn't about us anymore. It's about the children.

Did I say children? I meant child. Let's take this creating-life thing one hypothetically fertilized egg at a time.

• •

trip tip

Why It's Better to be You Than Gwen Stefani

THE MINUTE YOU BEGIN TRYING to conceive, something bizarre happens: Every other (female) celebrity on the planet suddenly is spotted shopping for a $3,000 retro-style British pram. It's true. As I'm patiently waiting for each period not to appear, I am bombarded with images of delicately swelling icons. Almost simultaneously, Gwyneth, Sarah Jessica, Brooke, Julia, Angelina, Britney, Courtney, Reese and the Kates (Hudson and Winslet) are in the family way. Six-pack abs are out and burgeoning bellies are in! Rotund tummies are the new Birkin bag, and mine's on backorder.

At first you might feel a special kinship with these women, but then you realize that's an absurd notion. Why? Because these women are not actually human, so comparing yourself and your pregnancy to theirs is like comparing your bank account or botox-free brow line to theirs. When you are twelve weeks pregnant and you look like John Goodman, it does nothing for your already fragile ego to see photos of Prada-clad kabillionaires with popsicle-stick bodies who are twice as far along as you are.

Here's what we all need to remember: Celebrities have a team of overpriced personal trainers and live-in chefs monitoring their every move and morsel to make sure they gain exactly the least amount of "healthy" baby weight possible. (Except for Catherine Zeta-Jones and Debra Messing, both of whom appeared to be pushing maximum density at the end— and looking radiant, healthy and gorgeous in the process, I might add. Alas, even these relative heifers were back into their size negative-four jeans five minutes after giving birth, so you can still hate them.) Celebrities also have publicists who, I would guess, sometimes make up fictitious due dates, so maybe when the photo says "Julia Roberts at eight months pregnant" (and she looks like she might be a bit gassy), maybe she's only four months along. Rumor has it many gestating starlets even request—and are granted—early inductions to avoid putting on those last few dozen pesky pounds.

Do not, however, harbor any resentment toward these women. Think of all the things you have that they don't: When you gain sixty-five pounds and no longer have a discernable neck, your puffy face will not be plastered on the

trip tip

covers of hundreds of international tabloid magazines. When your child emerges from your body, you don't have to worry about some paparazzi lowlife lurking in the hospital bushes trying to snap and sell the first photos for millions of dirty dollars; you can traipse down to Sears Portrait Studio and get started for as little as $4.99. You won't have to kill yourself trying to string together random letters of the alphabet in an effort to make up the strangest and most ridiculous baby name in creation. John, Jake, Allison and Amanda are lovely names! You can pick one that already exists and be done with it. You probably won't be asked to pose in *Playboy's* "Yummy Mummy" spread or saunter down a Victoria's Secret runway in your barely there, diamond-encrusted skivvies a mere eight weeks after delivery. (And while I'm sure Heidi Klum is a nice person, I hope for your sake she's not in your mommy-and-me class.) My sister tells me "nine months on, nine months off" is a sensible, feasible approach to pregnancy weight gain. It's times like this that you really appreciate that your sister isn't Uma Thurman.

Even though you have all of these reasons to be glad you're not, say, Cindy Crawford, and even though you are going to temporarily suspend your subscriptions to *Us, People* and *Star,* you're bound to catch a glimpse of an expecting supernova at some point during your efforts to procreate. When you do, you may be gripped with envy and resentment. In honor of the Buddhist practice of mindful meditation, I suggest recognizing these thoughts and feelings, writing them down and then letting them go. It really is the healthy, tolerant thing to do. And because we're in this together, I'll walk you through it.

Find a quiet, serene place where you can think and compose freely. Take a few deep breaths, and conjure the beautiful images of all of the famous fertile females whose likenesses are being broadcast around the globe right this minute. Allow your affection and admiration for them to spin and swirl around you like a magnificent white light. Now, begin to list:

Expecting non-water-retaining celebrities with only one chin and delicate ankles who don't even look pregnant from the back that I fantasize about kidnapping and forcing to eat sixteen triple-fudge sundaes:

1. _____
2. _____
3. _____
4. _____
5. _____
6. _____
7. _____
8. _____
9. _____
10. _____
11. _____
12. _____
13. _____
14. _____
15. _____

trip tip

3

....

He Shoots, He Scores!

Y ou know how everyone tells you not to tell anyone that you're trying to get pregnant? At first I thought this was simple common courtesy, as if by not disclosing this little nugget you are sparing your friends and relatives from picturing all of that valiant, clumsy endeavoring. I quickly learn the real wisdom behind this advice: The minute you tell folks you are "trying," the pressure is on.

"Well?" they drawl each time you see them, sizing you up to see if there's any noticeable addition to your girth.

"Nothing yet," you reply as breezily as you can. You resist the urge to share such details as precisely when your period hit this month, what you were wearing (white pants, invariably) when it did and how you sobbed for three days afterward over the loss of your potential progeny. You'd already done the math, you see: "If I get pregnant this month, the baby will be born sometime in mid-April. Oh, a spring baby! What could be more perfect? I won't have to be hugely pregnant when it's ungodly hot out and I'll be back in shape by Labor Day!" (You are, of course, too naive at this point to realize that if you did have that baby in April, you'd then be lugging a sweaty newborn and her copious necessities around all sizzling summer long, which is no bloody picnic either, and that—as anyone who has been dieting for the better part of her life knows—five months is not a lot of time to take off fifty or so pounds. But I digress.)

You will get sick of the status checks because you will feel like a colossal failure every time you have to report that your uncooperative, inconsiderate womb is not yet playing hostess to an embryo. One month will feel like one hundred, and after ninety torturous days without success you will force your husband to endure the humiliation of having his sperm count checked. While he's busy bragging to all of his buddies about his 500 million swimmers, you will call your gynecologist and ask if you should undergo some tests of your own. She will assure you that it can take six months to a year for perfectly healthy couples to conceive. But you don't want to wait that long. You're not the layaway type. You want this now, and if something is wrong with you, you want to know immediately.

When all of the tests turn out okay (and obviously sometimes they don't—but by "you" I mean "me," and hate me if you will, but apparently I didn't get birthing hips for nothing), you will relax a bit. You will go back to the grind, so to speak, with renewed gusto. As each potential period approaches, you will once again begin envisioning your increasingly swollen self at every upcoming holiday, celebration and milestone if this is indeed the month your little egg gets lucky. ("At least I won't be a Mac truck at Pam's wedding," you'll think, "but *what on earth* am I going to wear for New Year's Eve?") You will calculate the enormous pile of dough you will save not buying tampons ("Two boxes a month at $7 a box times ten months…whoa, that's $140!"), not realizing you will spend twice the net savings the first month you're pregnant on new, unscented shampoo and anti-nausea ginger chews. You'll look at your body in the mirror—sideways—a lot, trying to imagine what it will look and feel like when it has a living creature the size of a toaster inside of it.

Above all, you will have sex, and lots of it. You will do it when you don't feel like it; when there's laundry to fold and there are bills to pay, pets to feed and work to be done; when you're angry and tired and haven't shaved your legs in a week, even during your period, because "you never know." Since your partner long ago stopped assisting with the legs-in-the-air part, you will do this yourself while he shuffles to the kitchen to make himself a salami sandwich. You will exercise gently but regularly. You will meditate and visualize and practice deep-breathing exercises that make you light-headed and queasy. You will make lists of baby names, mentally design the nursery and obsess over clever possible headlines for the birth announcement. You might even go to a maternity shop and buy some clothes, just so you're ready. (Maybe not, but I did this. I even staged a fashion show for Joe, using his basketball as a bump. Yes, I looked pathetic and absurd, but I was excited just by the fact that I was excited—and by not mocking me or even shaking his head sadly, Joe proved to me that he would make a wonderful and supportive father.) You will go from enjoying the occasional glass of wine to a life of smug sobriety because you are committed to the cause *that much*. When friends call to announce their pregnancies, you will bite your tongue until you taste the salty blood, and gush and giggle and wish them well. You will pray to a god you're not sure you believe in and make outrageous promises involving daily devotional sessions if He or She could please, just this once, find it in his or her heart to grant you this teeny, tiny wish. You will read books about pregnancy to prepare yourself. You will read books about parenting to make sure you really know what you're getting into (and occasionally, to comfort yourself when the pregnancy test comes back negative). You will keep taking your temperature, scrutinizing your bodily secretions and engaging in perfunctory, kissing-less sunrise sex. And miraculously one day, this:

You're squatting over your toilet, attempting to direct your urine flow onto a small plastic stick's impossibly tiny plastic window. Pee drips down your hand, a fact that once would have made you gag, but now seems utterly immaterial. You place the stick on the counter, wash your hands and wait. Five minutes feels longer than a transatlantic flight in coach class. You re-read the test directions for the thirty-seventh time, just to be sure.

Any line, no matter how faint, indicates pregnancy.

You stare at the miniature window until your eyes burn, but nothing happens. *It's broken,* you think angrily, checking the expiration date on the package. Still good. You return to staring at the stick, trying not to blink. But the harder you focus on keeping your eyes open, the stronger the urge to close them becomes. Finally you can't resist a quick flutter. When your eyes readjust, you think you may see the faintest whisper of a line beginning to appear. You blink again, wait for your eyes to focus and right there on the screen is a pale, pale stripe. It's barely visible, in fact, but it's definitely there if you squint. And holy mother of Jesus, even if you don't.

Any line, no matter how faint…

You're pregnant. You place your hand gently, reverently, on your abdomen. *There's a person in there. A teeny, tiny person. In there!* You don't know whether to laugh or to cry. You pace around your living room. You sit and look around the empty room helplessly. Aren't you supposed to be *doing* something? (Besides going to church; that can wait a day or two. God will understand.) Oh yes! Your husband! He should know, too! But you've spent months devising the world's most perfect, clever, sentimental method of breaking this monumental news ever devised. The kangaroo costume is on hold, the tiny porcelain baby booties—small enough to fit inside the neck of a beer bottle—are stashed in the back of the pantry, along with the "Baby on Board" suction-cup car window decal you found (gently used) at a garage sale.

You manage to wait an impressive forty-two seconds before caving in and dialing your husband's direct line at work. When you get his voicemail, you hang up. You could call your sister or your mother or your best friend, but your husband would be furious (and rightly so) if he wasn't the first to know. Your "Hey, Daddy" skywriting fantasies fly right out the window as you quickly redial. "Hi, it's me," you blurt out after the beep. "Um, I'm just calling because…we're…well, I'm… pregnant. Okay, so…call me."

It's okay, really. Not everyone is great under pressure. This doesn't mean you won't make a good mom. Honest.

The wait for him to call you back is eternal. You sit and you stand and you pace and you wring your hands and you try to figure out what to do with your new, expectant self. Your body, however, already seems to be on autopilot. It leads you into your car and to the nearest drive-thru, where it thoughtfully orders you the most delicious cheeseburger you have ever eaten in your life. (Never mind that you don't eat meat and haven't touched so much as a single fast-food ketchup packet in more than a decade.) And a vanilla milkshake because ice cream has protein and babies need protein! You order another burger to go, ostensibly for your husband, but you eat that one, too. You don't feel even the slightest twinge of guilt about this because you're eating for two now. Your new mission in life is actually to *gain* weight. So far, this pregnancy thing isn't so bad after all.

- -

trip tip

Not Every Burp
Belongs in the Baby Book

UNLESS YOU ARE ONE of the three virgin brides who tie the knot every year, chances are you have spent years—possibly decades—doing everything within your power (except abstaining from sex, which clearly would be extreme) to avoid the very situation in which you now find yourself. My heartfelt congratulations! Perhaps you've already started some sort of diary—cataloging every delicious, rapturous moment of this delightful period. If that's the case, forge on! And good for you, really. Alas, there may be times when you'd like to commemorate some of the less-pleasant episodes (few as surely they will be!) of gestation—if for no other reason than to reflect back on them, should you ever decide to travel this euphoric road again. ("Hmmm," you'll muse wistfully. "Did I get those hemorrhoids in the first or second trimester last time?" Believe it or not, you may not recall every such titillating detail after a few months or years have passed.) Use this space to jot down those notes you'd rather your unborn child not stumble upon when perusing his future baby book:

I plan to gain _____ pounds over the course of my pregnancy.

(I actually gained _____ pounds [multiply above number by 3.5 for a rough estimate]. My partner gained _____ pounds.)*

My naked pregnant body looks like (a priceless sculpture, a lithe muscular snake lying atop a small ripe orange, a sausage that swallowed a misshapen hippopotamus, two hundred pounds of flesh-toned cottage cheese wedged into a one hundred-pound stocking, etc.) _____

_____

_____

Wow! I'm amazed at my insatiable appetite for (fried calamari, wonton soup, sparkling lemonade, abstinence, triple-fudge sundaes, etc.) _____

_____

_____

Before getting pregnant, I wanted to have _____ baby/babies.

Now I want _____ baby/babies.

When my partner makes that "So, ya feeling frisky?" face, I (ignore him, play the morning sickness card, stay at my mother's for a week, give him the evil look that's come to mean *That's what got us into this mess in the first place, asshole,* etc.) _____

_____

_____

_____

*Fill this part out later. Or make something up. Or black it out with a fat marker and pretend you spilled some sort of stinky herbal tea here.

trip tip

Unpleasant side effects of pregnancy I am experiencing that friends warned me about:_____

_____

_____

Unpleasant side effects of pregnancy I am experiencing that *no one* warned me about:_____

_____

_____

_____

My initial thought when I saw the first ultrasound photo of my baby was ("S/he is even more beautiful than I could have imagined," "Whoa, hope those webs between his/her feet go away," "Holy smokes, I was impregnated by an alien," etc.) _

_____

_____

_____

_____

_____

My bra size has gone from a _____ to a _____ during this pregnancy.

[To be filled in on baby's first birthday] My breasts, which used to resemble _____, now look more like _____.

When no one is looking, I sneak into the kitchen and eat

_____

_____

_____

_____

_____

_____

_____

_____

_____

_____

_____

_____

_____

_____

I plan to lose the baby weight in _____ weeks/months/ years. (I actually lost the baby weight in _____ weeks/ months/years/still waiting.)

trip tip

Parenting phrases my own parents used that I swear on my childhood cat's grave to never, under any circumstances—not even if I am forced to watch twenty-seven back-to-back episodes of SpongeBob SquarePants—utter to my child or children ("Because I said so!" "This hurts me more than it hurts you," "As long as you live under my roof you will abide by my rules," etc.):** _____

_____

_____

_____

_____

_____

_____

_____

_____

_____

** This bit intentionally given its own page so that it can be carefully removed with no trace should the unlikely need arise.

4

....

The Rehearsal Dinner— or the Entire Wedding?

The first thing I do when I find out I'm expecting—after washing down the aforementioned cheeseburgers with the universe's creamiest milkshake—is to promptly ignore all of that conventional "wait until twelve weeks" nonsense and call every single person I've ever met in my entire life and break the news. Who are the women who manage to wait four or even *fourteen* weeks before divulging this? It's all I can think about. I find a way to mention it to every person I so much as make eye contact with, from the mailman ("Oh, my *Fit Pregnancy* magazine hasn't come yet? Darn...it's just that now that I'm pregnant...") to the stranger in line behind me at the grocery store ("You're buying Brie! Lucky you. I love the stuff, but no unpasteurized cheese for me..."). When I can't find a way to bring it up, I rub my still-level belly and smile idiotically until someone—anyone—gives me the raised eyebrow. "Yup," I nod sagely, as if I created the idea of creating life. "Pregnant."

And here's the thing: Your whole life you hear about the "miracle of childbirth." You might even have used the phrase once or twice, but you never really gave it much thought, much the way you might throw around sayings like "dog day afternoon" or "fit to be tied." But the minute you discover that your very own body is housing the delicate beginnings of a human life, you begin to consider the true unlikelihood of it all. That a sperm you never even saw—and could never see even if you tried—penetrated an egg you weren't sure you had is pretty unlikely. Even if you can accept that implausibility, the fact that your insides just know what to do all by themselves and then proceed to do it is a sheer, unmitigated wonder. But the part that blows me away the most is that this *person* you create will walk and talk, and possibly do karaoke, and hopefully vote and pay taxes, and maybe even run a marathon or run for public office, and definitely have her (okay, or his) very own thoughts and ideas that may or may not coincide with yours. This seems flat-out impossible. Miraculous, if you will.

To prepare for this supernatural occurrence, the next thing I do is stock up on books. There is no shortage of options, so I arm myself with a few technical tomes of the week-by-week and month-by-month variety, several celebrity tell-alls and a ludicrous selection of baby name guides. Of course I need a pregnancy organizer—not to be confused with a pregnancy journal, which I also purchase—and a few volumes of words of wisdom especially for the expectant father. When I'm not looking, *Oh, Baby, the Places You'll Go! A Book to Be Read in Utero* leaps uninvited into my basket. If it's possible to get a PhD in procreating, I am well on my way.

The books are plenty enlightening and informative. But here's something I wish someone had suggested at the time: Get yourself a book on *babies*! Because the pregnancy part pretty much takes care of itself. You can be working, sleeping, playing tennis, growing corn, lobbying Congress, panning for gold or having sex (if you're so inclined; I find that I am usually too nauseous, hungry, tired or just plain uncomfortable to do the deed, although I know several women who say pregnancy hormones turn them into horndogs), and it matters not. Assuming that you are not mainlining heroin or knocking back your weight in tequila every night, your body is going to take care of business and put all of those tiny parts in place. Sure, it's nice to be up on your gestational trivia ("Oh look, honey! We made a brain this week!"). But your unborn offspring will not pop out clutching a user's manual, and despite the fact that you have never kept so much as a cactus alive, you will be expected to know how and when to feed, bathe, burp, swaddle, nurse, hold, rock, walk, diaper and soothe her. A little educational perusing during this endless waiting period can do wonders to boost your confidence.

While I could fill several thousand pages detailing every bloated moment of my endless pregnancy, I am going to share but a few of the most memorable ones. Part of the reason for this is that everyone's experience is as different as the one-of-a-kind babies they produce. You might genuinely love every minute of the magical reproduction process. You might feel stronger and healthier and sexier than you have ever felt at any other time in your life. (If you do, I promise to try really hard to be nice to you if we ever meet.) But the bigger reason is that while you're in it, pregnancy truly seems like the destination. Untold numbers of books out there will tell you precisely how to do it and how to feel while you're doing it (and I know this for a fact because I now own them all). But for the most part, reading them while pregnant is sort of like perusing a book on aerospace engineering while you sip a vodka and tonic on a flight to Lisbon: There might be lots of handy navigational tips, but you're really just along for the ride. The truth is, gestation is a journey. The actual destination is parenthood, and that's another trip altogether. And since it's a much longer voyage and, it turns out, a hell of a lot more entertaining, that's the one I really want to talk about.

Still, if getting there is half the fun, at the moment I'm a little concerned about where I'm headed. By my fifth week of pregnancy (at which point the embryo has only been in there for three weeks, but for some unknown reason "they" count your pregnancy from the first day of your *last* period, even though it's pretty clear you weren't pregnant then), I am as sick as a dog—assuming that dog swallowed a live porcupine and washed it down with a gallon of radiator fluid. Morning sickness, my ass. This particular breed of nausea wears no watch and just about the only thing that puts even the tiniest dent in it is massive quantities of food.

So I eat. Pretty much constantly. Corndogs and pizza and tacos and ginger snaps and meatballs and anything that's not chicken or green. "Try to eat a balanced diet" goes the standard OB refrain. She might as well say "Establish world peace" for both its practicality and probability. "You're not going to have dessert? You *have* to have dessert!" cries your waiter, and of course, he is right. You *do* have to have dessert. You deserve it. Since you can't smoke or drink or scuba dive or go snowboarding (even though you never did most of those things anyway), you might as well enjoy the occasional crème brûlée.

If you stick to your round-the-clock consumption schedule, you will start packing on the pounds. Your blossoming will rank up there on the hottest dinner party topic list with how much so-and-so recently made in the real estate market. Your weight goes from a number whose secrecy you once guarded as if it were the holy grail to something they write with *a fat red marker* on the outside of your medical folder. "How much have you gained?" perfect strangers will ask. *None of your effing business* you will think as you toss out whatever phony number you have decided in advance sounds reasonable.

I am actually surprised that tripling my typical food intake is only adding up to about an extra pound a week. (When I do this on vacation,

I can always count on packing on a good seven or eight pounds.) By week twenty, I look like I've been on vacation for about two months too many. Even though I've added eighteen pounds to my frame, I am still not sporting that cute pregnancy profile you see on greeting cards and maternity clothes labels. Instead, my abdomen seems to be growing outward instead of forward, making me look like I am carrying this baby in a partially inflated inner tube around my waist.

At least there's a booby prize. Two of them, to be precise. A mere four months ago, if you'd ever seen a pair of deviled eggs on a platter, you had all but seen me naked from the waist up. Now, however, while I'm not waiting for *Penthouse* to bang my door down, I could definitely give one of the lesser Victoria's Secret models a run for her stockings. The wonder twins are a welcome sight.

"Can I touch them?" Joe asks eagerly, eyeing my new curves and reaching for me with the familiar tune-in-Tokyo double grab.

"Do it and die," I growl, shrinking away from him. It feels as if every nerve ending I possess has relocated to the region right smack in the middle of my areolas, making the whole heaving mass udderly— I mean utterly—untouchable. (Note to Alanis Morissette: Now *that's* ironic.)

As my next ultrasound appointment approaches, we are giddy with anticipation. *Of course* we're going to find out the sex. I cannot for the life of me fathom not wanting to know this crucial bit of information. "But your baby's sex is one of the greatest surprises of your life!" people try to convince us. We agree! And we're going to be fully surprised when we do find out. We also will have four and a half months to agree on a name, paint the nursery the appropriate color and convince ourselves that the sex we're getting is the one we wanted all along.

Because let's face it: Everyone has a preference. "I just want a healthy baby," people spit when posed the gender question, looking positively appalled that one would even ask what they "want." This is a universal lie. Okay, it's only a *partial* universal lie because the healthy part is probably pretty legit. No one wants to admit it, but deep down, most guys want a (healthy) boy and most women want a (healthy) girl. It's what we know! I have no problem admitting that I am absolutely unqualified to explain wet dreams and spontaneous erections to a ten-year-old boy, and I'd love to be a fly on the wall listening to Joe introduce his would-be daughter to her first box of Tampax or her inaugural training bra. Of course, there are exceptions—women who fantasize about raising a gentleman and men who dream of being worshipped by a "daddy's girl"—but either way, there's usually a partiality. I have admitted to Joe that I am hoping for a daughter (pedicures and ruffled panties and party dresses and pink hair ribbons!); he's confessed he'd love a son (basketball and G.I. Joe and fly fishing and dart guns!). Today we find out who wins this fateful coin toss.

Although my pregnancy is moving along swimmingly, it's standard operating procedure in our tiny town to have the hotshot high-risk OB do the midway ultrasound. Probably he's better at not only spotting problems, but also breaking bad news. Of course, we're not thinking about anything but penis or vagina. Blue or pink. Baseballs or ballerina slippers. Jake or Samantha. The rehearsal dinner or the entire wedding.

The doctor rubs the icy wand over my well-lubed belly. "Well?" we bark in unison.

"I'm getting there," he laughs. "Hmmm…."

Joe and I exchange panicked looks. Hmmm? What could that mean? Twins? A eunuch? *Twin eunuchs?*

The doctor senses our tension. "Everything looks great," he assures. "Beautiful spine, nice brain…see the chambers of the heart? Very nice… no sign of club foot, spina bifida, cleft palate…."

My heart stops beating while he continues rattling off a laundry list of horrors my mind honestly has never even contemplated. Sure, I've worried in those generic terms I mentioned ("I hope the baby is healthy"), but I purposely skipped all of the scary-complication chapters in my arsenal of books. I mean, why go there? If ignorance is bliss in everyday life, it's downright orgasmic when you're pregnant.

"So," he continues. "Want to know the sex?"

"Yes!" we shout, practically blowing the guy into next week with our excitement.

The doctor looks at me, then Joe, then back at me again.

"It's a girl," he almost whispers.

I can't look at Joe. I can't. They say it is physically impossible to feel happiness and sadness in the same moment, but at this instant I'd have to disagree. Imagine you say to your best friend, "I'll bet you a thousand bucks you break your leg today." When she does, it's not much of a victory for you. Man, did I ever want a girl. But even though we both know it's the man's sperm that dictates the gender, I still feel as if it is my fault, that I willed it—her—into having a vagina. I want to jump up and down and do an obnoxious little happy dance and name her on the spot and start planning our first tea party. But I try to put myself in Joe's shoes and imagine how I'd be feeling if I just found out she was a he.

Finally, I look at my husband. His sad smile nearly rips my heart out of my chest. "You okay?" I ask, hating him for a split second for taking away my joy.

"Of course I am," he says, shaking his head as if trying to convince himself of it. "I just need some time to get used to the idea."

I can't help it, I start crying. The doctor slips out of the room. "No one is ever going to love you like this little girl will," I whisper through my tears, wrapping my arms protectively around my middle.

I am thirty-three and still believe my own dad hung the moon in the sky for my personal viewing pleasure.

His eyes are wet, too. "I know," he says feebly.

"You won't have to do anything but exist and you've got it made. It's *me* she's going to fight with and resent and rebel against!" I add fiercely. "I'm actually jealous."

He pulls me into his arms and buries his face in my neck. "Yeah," he says with a sniffle and a soft laugh and just a touch of sarcasm. "It sucks to be you."

I don't really think that, I tell the universe, because I can be as new-agey as the next girl. I believe that thoughts are energy, and right now I am not taking any chances. I'm going to have a daughter, which means I'm going to need all the help I can get.

trip tip

Take my Husband. . . Please!

FOR MANY WOMEN, pregnancy is a hormonal roller-coaster ride. Even if the joyous highs consistently outnumber the agonizing, gut-wrenching lows, when you hit a trough you can be caught unaware. My lowest low comes the evening my (otherwise likable) husband actually says the following sentence. Out loud.

"I don't know if we should have any more kids."

Clearly I am in a dark and dangerous hormonal valley at the moment, because what follows (after the mother of all pregnant pauses) is anything but pretty.

"Any *more* kids?" I finally hiss with more venom than an angry cobra. "We don't even have *one* yet! And it's a little late in the game to be suggesting *this* one is a mistake, in case you hadn't noticed."

"What I mean is, I'm not really enjoying this pregnancy," he says seriously.

It's all I can do not to rip the beer bottle out of his hand and crack it over his skull.

"You're not *enjoying* it?" I spit, stuttering and stammering furiously. "*You're* not enjoying it? Really? Because it's a freaking joyride for me! I *love* dry-heaving into the toilet eleven times a day! I love that none of my clothes fit! I love feeling starving all the time even though I can't think of a single food that sounds palatable. I love that I can't sleep on my back, and let me tell you, decaf coffee is seriously underrated. That stuff's fantastic."

"This is *exactly* what I mean," he replies. "You're moody and unpredictable and sarcastic all the time. I never know how you're going to react to anything I say. I feel like I'm constantly walking on eggshells around here. I'm actually *scared* of you."

"Well, you should be!" I roar. "How *dare* you try to make this about you! Remind me, please, how your life has changed, other than this unfortunate lack of enjoyment you're experiencing, since *'we'* got pregnant. Because I forget."

"I used to be married to my best friend," he says sadly.

I am not telling you this story to depress you, honestly. But these can be trying times. You feel like you're sacrificing everything, while he's sacrificing, well, nothing. And even though you know it's for the greater good and you want this baby more than you have ever wanted anything in your whole life, you don't remember signing up for this particular cascade of events or emotions. At the very least, you wish someone would have *told* you that you'd feel like this. That you'd worry constantly about your ability to be a mother. That basic activities like sleeping and walking would suddenly feel foreign to you. Are you eating enough? Of the right foods? Maybe you shouldn't have that Coke, even though it tastes so good and your headache goes away the minute you take the first bubbly, satisfying gulp. And on top of it all, you have the flu, which is obviously your fault because you didn't get your flu shot this year. Now you feel like crap, but you can't take anything resembling medicine because it could harm the baby. So you suffer. And sulk. And as you watch your partner greedily swig from the NyQuil bottle like a bum sucking down bourbon, you think—for not the first time in recent memory—"I hate him."

You don't hate him. Not really. You hate yourself for not having the grace or the goodness to enjoy every nanosecond of your indigestion—I mean, pregnancy. Some women do, after all. You've met them, seen them, heard about them or (worst of all) might even be related to them. Unlike you, these women won't buy nine different brands of unscented organic soap in an effort to find one that doesn't make them gag, itch or both. They don't wake their partners in the middle of the night to regale them with every titillating detail of their most recent dream. They won't hire an exterminator to crawl through the attic and remove the rotting animal corpse that isn't there, even though they are convinced that it is. And they will never insist that the brand-new couch reeks of cat urine (even though their cat is too old and feeble to actually jump onto the couch) and force their husbands to drag the offensive piece of furniture into the garage.

I'm going to let you in on a maddeningly well-kept secret: You don't have to love being pregnant. You don't even have to like it. You just have to get through it without killing your partner. This can be accomplished by following a few basic guidelines:

- Never agree to be responsible for waking him up to catch his 5:00 a.m. flight. When it doesn't happen, he'll insist it's your fault because "you always do it," and even though you are extremely busy *making a person,* he won't see the logic in this. Not only will you be stuck looking at his sour puss the entire time he should have been gone, but

trip tip

trip tip

the resulting knock-down-drag-out will compound your already crippling exhaustion.

- It's okay to assemble an arsenal of pillows if they help you sleep more comfortably; just try to leave enough room on the bed for your partner. Soon enough you'll need him in there to help with the midnight feedings, so you don't want him getting too used to the couch or guest bed.

- Ask your partner to do things for you (scour the refrigerator, run you a bath, switch deodorant brands) that will make your life more pleasant. If you can manage to suggest an activity without telling him precisely *how* to do it, the odds of compliance will increase exponentially.

- When going out to eat, do your marriage a favor and pick the restaurant. Although the *least* he could do right now would be to develop superpowers, the reality is he probably won't instinctively know that the *chiles rellenos* you couldn't get enough of last week are likely to make you hurl today.

- Don't begrudge his inability to bear children. He didn't choose his anatomy any more than you chose yours. When your own swollen ankles are depressing you, remember that he has to walk around with an unpredictable penis all the time, which, as far as I can see, isn't particularly relaxing *or* fun.

- If you're going to have a baby shower, make it coed. Some women insist that this is a great way to get the dad-to-be involved and excited, but the real reason for this is that if you incorporate fun games like the "diaper Olympics" (where the guys race to properly diaper a doll), he might pick up a trick or two that will benefit *you* in the months and years ahead.

- Don't comment on his growing gut. Lots of guys pack on a few sympathy pounds during their wives' pregnancies (could you merely watch while he downed his weight in fudge brownies?). Pretend you don't notice it—even when he goes to excessive lengths to push it out, rub it lovingly and call it "his baby"—and he may reciprocate this time next year.

- When he makes annoying comments such as "You're going to break your ankle in those stupid shoes," try to remember that this is his way of expressing loving concern for you and the baby. Your obviously superior fashion sense has nothing whatsoever to do with it, so trying to argue that point will get you nowhere.

- Stop keeping score. There's nothing "fair" about pregnancy. Sure, if men had to do it, epidurals would come in a shot glass, maternity leave would last for years and someone, somewhere, would have developed a boob-lifting cream that actually works. But then again, you'd have to listen to *his* whiny, incessant ranting for ten torturous months. Remember that the next time you feel the urge to clock him.

trip tip

5

....

287 Days is a
Really, Really Long Time

All of my pregnancy books and magazines talk about it, and I can't wait for it to happen. Finally, overnight, I "pop." It sounds painful and messy, but this has nothing to do with springing an embarrassing leak. Instead, of its own accord my spare tire seems to have repositioned itself into that darling little forward-facing half-melon configuration most often associated with my condition. Although it seems to have magnetic properties where food is concerned (was I always such a slob?), I love my hard little belly with every fiber in my being. Plus, I finally feel officially pregnant.

"Have you felt her kick yet?" This question ranks up there with the weight-gain query among curious onlookers. The truth is I am not sure. Friends alternately tell me it will feel like "butterfly wings fluttering against my insides," "tiny, almost imperceptible hiccups" and "hunger pangs even though I know I'm not hungry." Which is silly, of course, because I can't for the life of me recall what it feels like not to be hungry.

Eventually, however, the rumblings become unmistakable. Each time I feel a nudge, it takes my breath away. No matter what I'm doing,

I am immediately reminded of my greater purpose at the moment: I am a human incubator. As ridiculous as it seems and even though it is the most natural thing in the world, the fact that there is a body inside of my body never ceases to floor me.

But even when your pregnancy is unburdened by tiresome orders to stay in bed and watch TiVo'd *Oprah* reruns all day, if you try really hard you can still manage to find things to complain about. While I am grateful every day that my body clearly was designed to reproduce, I find that I can only be buoyed by the occasional internal jab for so long. By week thirty it feels like I have been pregnant forever. My feet hurt, my back aches and I am exhausted, bloated and bitter. My inconsequential but nonetheless irritating list of grievances includes, but is not limited to, random bloody noses, a constant low-grade head-ache, embarrassing and uncontrollable flatulence, a vile yeast infection that's taken over my mouth, constant searing sciatic pain, a chest that suddenly looks like a road map thanks to a network of broken blood vessels that have sprung up from neck to nipples and the urgent need to urinate at fifteen-minute intervals around the clock.

"I'm done," I moan to my husband. Forget about the mysterious pregnancy glow; if I'm even remotely radiant it's because my once-trim frame's thirty-plus new pounds cause me to sweat like a linebacker almost constantly. My legs form a straight line from feet to knees, I can no longer shave my bikini line myself (and while Joe and I both at one time considered it foreplay when I handed the razor over to him, now it seems downright pitiful) and my neck and armpits appear to be pregnant with tiny dermal babies of their very own. Compounding the insult, this repulsive constellation of "skin tags" costs sixty bucks a piece to be snipped off by my dermatologist, a maddening fact when you consider the surgical amputation of a skin tag requires roughly the same deftness and experience as clipping the price tag off of a new pair of panties. (Sure, I *could* attempt to do this myself, but when you are perpetually on the verge of vomiting, cutting off bits of your own flesh is definitely not an option.) I want to jump on a trampoline, paint my own toes, do Pilates, talk on the phone without getting winded, go braless, eat Caesar salad and sashimi and chocolate-covered espresso beans, lie on my stomach, slather my skin with glycolic acid and not have to wait until Joe comes home to deal with the stinking pile of cat poo in the litter box. I want to meet my daughter. I want to hold, kiss, dress, rock, coo over and cuddle her. I want to say her name out loud. And I really, *really* want a margarita.

"I'm sorry, honey," he soothes. "What can I do to make it better?"

"Get a vasectomy?" I am only half-joking. I don't know how I could ever willingly go through this again. I think about the mothers who do this four, ten, fourteen times over—sometimes *on purpose*—and the surrogate moms who "enjoy" the process of pregnancy so much they offer their wombs up as living test tubes for babies who won't even spring for their nursing home bills one day. An unthinkable thought flutters through my brain: *I'd better really like this kid.* Joe tells me there's no such thing as a living martyr, but I feel like I am proof to the contrary.

To take my mind off of my discomfort, I work on compiling a baby registry, a task that turns out to be nearly as daunting as the pregnancy itself. Do we need six bottles or sixty? Two crib sheets or two hundred? A basic stroller, a jogging model, the umbrella style, one with a convertible seat or an entire "travel system?" Is the $700 two-way digital video monitor with built-in temperature alert system and video recording capabilities a tad excessive or an absolute must?

When we finally get the registry compiled, another handy distracton comes along in the form of our prenatal birth preparation class. It occurs to me in the very first meeting that one way or another, in the not-too-distant future I am going to be expected to move this baby from the inside to the outside of my body. Now, you might assume that I knew this all along, and on some subconscious level I am pretty sure that I did. But the painfully frank banter about episiotomies and emergency cesarean sections brings on a fresh wave of nausea.

It's no help that I live in a very progressive community where drug-free deliveries are trendy and saving the placenta to make healing tinctures with—or eat—are not uncommon practices. Of the ten women in the room, I am the lone lily-liver who does not request additional information on water birthing, is so conservative that she feels compelled to invite a doctor of medicine into her delivery room and is extreme enough not just to demand an epidural, but to refuse to push if she isn't given one.

"I'll feel robbed if I don't get to experience the beauty of a natural delivery," one granola bemoans, actual tears forming in the corners of her eyes. Really? Because I could easily turn into a bitter hag if this whole process hurts half as much as I suspect it's going to.

We get lots of handy tips in the class, some of which I actually pay attention to. But deep down inside, I have a sinking feeling that no particular combination of *hee-hee-hoo-hoo* is going to make those famously agonizing contractions any more sufferable.

Women squat in fields and pop out babies, I remind myself. *My mom never attended a Lamaze class. It's going to happen with or without this information.* This last thought is less comforting than the others.

In week thirty-six, my semi-monthly OB appointments get bumped up to weekly visits. I know all of the nurses in the office by name, and frequently we gossip and giggle so much I forget why I'm there in the first place. Not today.

"Hi Jenna!" they chime cheerfully in unison as I lumber into the waiting room.

"I'm done," I reply. They laugh knowingly.

"I'm done," I repeat to my doctor. This is my new refrain.

"You have four more weeks!" she cackles. I want to punch her in the teeth.

"But my mom and sister both had all of their babies by this point," I argue. "And I have a twenty-three-day cycle, and I read that short menstrual cycles correspond with short pregnancies."

"First babies rarely come early," she sing-songs. Yeah, well, sweat-soaked pregnant ladies rarely beat up infuriating gynecologists, but that's not to say it can't happen.

Back at home, I wallow in my discomfort. I notice with no small amount of alarm that the watch that once floated about my wrist like a delicate bracelet now leaves ugly indentations in my engorged flesh. My bladder feels as if a minivan is parked on top of it, I have no desire to exercise (in fact, I have an acute and overwhelming desire *not to* exercise) and even the short waddle to the bathroom is uncomfortable. I am the Badyear Blimp.

I stay up all night (might as well, I certainly can't sleep) researching methods believed to stimulate labor naturally. Although I refuse to resort to drinking castor oil—the diarrhea-and-delivery cocktail does not interest me in the slightest—I decide that acupuncture and some nice, strategic foot massages can't hurt. I eat salads drowning in balsamic vinegar and actually consume an entire repulsive pan of fried cauliflower. We hike the hill behind our house nightly, go out of our way to drive bumpy back roads and have lots of (awkward, utilitarian) sex. Still, no stork.

What could she possibly be waiting for, I wonder, cursing my over-accommodating womb. "No one's ever been pregnant forever," my doctor pithily replies at my thirty-nine-week bitchfest. This is not helpful. I have preregistered at the hospital, my bags are packed and the only thing missing from the nursery is an actual baby.

Then, out of nowhere, I get a little cramp. *Ouch,* I think, *that smarted.* Then another. And another and another, and praise the heavens and all their majesty, these things hurt! *Oh my God oh my God oh my God.* I dash to my computer and e-mail all of my friends and editors to inform them my maternity leave has officially started because *I am very clearly about to have a baby!* I stay up all night logging my contractions, but instead of getting stronger and closer together, they wane after two torturous days. I crawl into bed and sob, and even the diamond earrings my husband gives me can't lift my dismal spirits.

My due date comes and goes. I beg for an induction—I've been dying my hair for twenty years; what do I know about natural?—I want this kid *out* already. A battery of tests indicate all is well and that our stubborn little bundle still has plenty of amniotic fluid in which to float about. The only concern now is the possibility that she may soon reach a size more appropriate for a Thanksgiving turkey than a newborn baby. Finally, and without my even having to resort to physical threats, my doctor decides that it is time and schedules the blessed induction.

The magnitude of it all hits me like a cartoon anvil over the head: In two days, this baby will actually be on the *outside* of my body and— hallelujah!—I won't be pregnant anymore. In two days I will look into my daughter's face, a face I know intimately even though I have never laid eyes on it. In two days I will be someone's *mom.* I have no idea what that means, but I know my life will never be the same.

trip tip

Baby Registries are for the Greedy (and Other Dumb Thoughts You Might One Day Regret)

THERE ARE ONLY TWO gift-giving occasions in a person's life that I know of where one isn't merely permitted to select all of one's own swag, but is actively encouraged to do so. The occasions, of course, are when you announce to the world that you are about to have lots of legal, conjugal sex, and then again when you broadcast that all of your heroic efforts have paid off. (And even though these two events often occur within a few years' proximity to one another, isn't it mind-boggling how quickly your material wish list can change? One day, nothing suits your lifestyle more aptly than an assortment of cut-crystal serving platters and enough martini glasses to liquor up a dozen of your dearest friends. The next day, you're in the market for plastic sheet protectors and a state-of-the-art rectal thermometer.) The crazy thing in each of these instances is that you really can choose anything you'd like. I've seen leaf blowers, stepladders, massage gift certificates and blue chip stocks on various wedding registries, and once, a $23,000 "playhouse"—complete with running water, working interior and exterior lights and a flat-screen TV—on a baby registry. (I hope they liked the burp cloths we got them!)

Unless you are wealthy beyond any reasonable measure and the only thing you truly need for your unborn child is a play structure that is more elaborately equipped than the average American home, I would suggest registering for the necessities. This isn't a simple task for a number of reasons,

trip tip

the least of which being that it is difficult to determine what your needs will be before you actually have them. Fortunately, many stores and web sites offer handy checklists for expectant parents to use as a guide. (In this instance, "handy" is often synonymous with "absurd." But at least it's a start.)

My expecting friends Mariaelena and Stewart recently drove forty miles to the nearest Babies "R" Us because, well, babies are them so obviously that they have everything people who are about to birth a small person could need. This turned out to be true—and then some.

"We walked around in circles for two hours with the little scanner thingy," Mariaelena confesses glumly.

"Why are there forty-seven different kinds of highchairs?" Stewart demands. "And why do they range from thirty to *three hundred* dollars? Don't they all basically do the same job?"

Why indeed.

Feeling like they needed to fulfill their stated mission, Mariaelena and Stewart registered for...a sheet. One solid white, standard-issue, cotton crib sheet. Then they went out for ice cream. "I just couldn't handle the *pressure*," Mariaelena admits. "It was overwhelming."

The alternative to registering for baby stuff is *not* registering for baby stuff, which is a wonderful idea for folks who need seventy-two receiving blankets, the default off-the-rack baby gift.

So you need to register, which in the past necessitated at least one but in all likelihood several trips to your local baby superstore, each of which is only slightly less enjoyable than having your teeth scraped. But thankfully, we live in the electronic age. Expecting parents now can sit in the comfort of their own home—where one of the two can enjoy an icy malt beverage and neither is forced to wield a scanner thingy—and choose the items with which they will soon be showered.

You basically have two options when it comes to registering online. You can do weeks or months of painstaking research until you nail down the top-rated product in each of the zillions of baby-gear categories. Or you can let a few perfect strangers do all of the bothersome legwork for you.

Here's how it works: Type "baby registry" into a Google search. At the time of this writing, you will receive slightly more than seven million matches by doing this, but you'll probably only actually visit three or four thousand of them, so don't be overwhelmed. Click on one of the biggies—say, Target or Amazon—and then pretend you are searching for a pregnant friend's registry. At Babies"R"Us, for instance, you need only a last name to see someone's list. Type in Smith or Roberts and you're bound to strike registry gold.

Once you have found a selection of wish lists, peruse a few of them quickly. At first the items may be meaningless to you. "What the *hell* is a 'Velboa Snuzzler'?" you'll wonder, and justifiably so. Just keep scanning. After five or six you'll begin to notice some overlap. "Hey, Abby and Jerome in Illinois are getting the Original Wonder Bear with Silkie Trim! Karin and Josh in South Dakota want that, too!" You'll soon get to the point where you realize that the Sure Comfort Deluxe Newborn-to-Toddler Tub is clearly the only way to go, and that only morons aren't lining up to buy the Express II Microwave Steam Sterilizer with Auto-Timer Plus.

When something looks familiar, jot it down on the next page. Each time an item appears on another registry, make a check mark next to it. When the computer glare renders you completely cross-eyed and you can no longer perform

trip tip

trip tip

your due diligence, hand this book to your partner and ask him to create an online registry from your notes. Send him specifically to one of the mega-stores with generous return policies, because it might be four or five years before you are organized and energized enough to return the 137 things you will never open/use. The bright side of this is that by then, you'll probably have another two or three or seven kids, and although you will no longer care whether your follow-up off-spring have fluffy new blankets or stylish, gender-appropriate clothing, the store credit will come in handy for the truckload of diapers they'll go through each month.

Happy shopping!

Stuff We Aren't Entirely Sure We Need But That Lots of Other People Want: _____

_____

_____

_____

_____

_____

_____

_____

_____

_____

_____

_____

_____

6

....

This Just in: They Don't Call It *Labor* for Nothing

For the entire *ten months* I have been pregnant, just about every woman I encounter who has tread the path of incubation before me insists upon recounting her own birthing story. The more gruesome and violent the experience, the more enthusiastically she shares.

"Congratulations," Veteran Mom says, smiling wistfully and eyeing my bloated belly. "I just hope you have an easier time delivering than I did with little Wolfgang...."

I hear tales of vomiting, umbilical cord catastrophes, hospital lamps being hurled at husbands and doctors and nurses and even one perfectly innocent flower delivery guy, passing out (usually dads), pooping on the delivery table (almost always moms), babies getting stuck in birth canals, the nauseating stench of cauterized flesh, thirteen-inch needles, failed epidurals, drug mix-ups, vacuum extractor misfortunes, infected incisions and unexpected power outages. (I'm only telling you what other women told *me*. I'm not trying to scare you, honest. I'm pretty sure none of these things will happen to you.) Despite the gory stories, somehow I still cling to the hope that my delivery will be a snap. My older sister swears her second "slid out like a wet bar of soap," so between my clearly superior birthing genes (never mind that same sister's forty-hour first labor nightmare) and the visualization techniques I have been thinking about practicing, why shouldn't it be?

The answer to that is one word: Pitocin. Saying induction drugs intensify contractions is like saying half a bottle of Valium enhances a buzz. I won't tell you how long the hellish pain of labor lasts (but I will say this: I now consider the twelve-hour flight from L.A. to London a puddle jump) or go into any kind of detail regarding the copious volume of bodily fluids I surrender that day. Here's what I will tell you (and again, I am just one person and every woman is different; if you'd like to pen *your* tale I'd love nothing more than to read it):

1. Birthing balls suck. A friend suggested bringing one of these ginormous rubber bouncy things into the delivery room, ostensibly because bobbing on them is supposed to relieve some of the pain of labor by providing "counterpressure." This is absolute nonsense. Imagine someone is trying to force a watermelon, say, into your vagina. Or perhaps out of it. When the eight-pound fruit is just about in (or out), another person wraps a length of barbed wire around your midsection and periodically gives it a malicious tug. Can you for the life of you imagine how bouncing on a large rubber ball would provide any pain relief whatsoever? Precisely. It doesn't. Save the thirty bucks and spend it on a stockpile of medicated pads (more on that in a sec).

2. It doesn't matter one microscopic bit what "stage" you are in when you're giving birth. Our well-meaning prenatal instructor talked endlessly about early labor and active labor and transmission or transgression (or whatever it's called)—and I forget all of the other stages, but I think there were several more. And that's my point.

At no time when I am struggling to push that metaphorical camel through the eye of my literal vulva am I thinking *Hey! This must be active labor! Wonder when we'll get to transmigration?* My one and only thought is *Holy bleep! Where's the lady with the bleeping drugs?* Sorry to be so blunt, but that's how it goes. My advice: Forget about stages and reserve the brain space for the 3,429 nursery rhyme lyrics you're going to be reciting around the clock starting tomorrow.

3.   Don't turn your baby's birth into a party. This has nothing whatsoever to do with modesty. By the time thirty-two perfect strangers—a new nurse every eight hours, random interns, the occasional orderly and a parade of food and flower delivery people—have gotten a glimpse of your goods, you will never again consider those parts "private." But please trust me when I tell you that there is nothing more annoying than listening to an assembly of your most beloved friends and family members discussing this week's *American Idol* upset while you dry-heave into a kidney-shape dish. And some people, I've found, can get their little feelings hurt when you ask them gently if they might *pretty, pretty please shut the blank up already.*

4.   Everyone lies to the pregnant lady. Be prepared for this. "You're almost there!" they'll shout, and you'll be stupid and hopefully drugged enough to believe them. So you'll suck in the biggest breath your lungs can hold, grit your teeth through the agony, bear down and focus like they told you to do and push with a power and determination you didn't know you possessed. Four hours later when you hear someone say "The doctor is on her way," it will occur to you that the whole sorry lot of them have

been lying to you all along, but because it was for your own good and at least a handful of them might babysit for free, eventually you will forgive them.

5. You know that Barbie you had when you were a kid—the pregnant one whose belly popped off like a battery cover, allowing you to remove the peanut-size plastic baby and then snap on a flat new front (sold separately)? Well, that's not exactly how it works. Several hours after giving birth, I hobble to the nurses' station to refill my beloved bucket of ice chips. "Good luck," whispers a cute, somewhat disheveled twenty-something guy leaning against the counter. He winks at me, and for the life of me I don't get what he's saying. Surely he can't be hitting on me; I still have *vomit* in my hair. But good luck with what? With trying to get some more ice? With my life in general? Good luck being a mom? Then I realize: I still look ten months pregnant. How could he possibly know there's no baby in my Superdome-size belly? He means good luck with the *delivery*. I shuffle back to my room and mentally pen a scathing letter to Mattel that I will never send but makes me feel better nevertheless.

6. The baby might come out of your vagina, but your rear end takes a mighty beating, too. I can't remember if any of my pregnancy books addressed this, but since it is such a significant part of the postpartum aftermath, I figure it's worth mentioning. Now, I've never wrapped my naked body in raw bacon and run through a field of starving, rabid wolverines, but I can't imagine that experience being any more frightening than the prospect of voiding one's bladder and bowels in the hours after giving birth. Forget diamonds; stool softener is a maternity ward resident's best friend (and if the facility you are in doesn't offer it to you, you should

definitely ask to speak to the head administrator directly). This was not disclosed to me in advance, but they will not let me leave the hospital until I have proven that I can produce both forms of waste material. The fact that a nurse is waiting outside my bathroom door for me to gather the evidence does nothing to encourage these otherwise natural functions. I ask her to come back in a half hour, then I take a deep breath and try to relax. She shouts through the door that if I can't pee she'll be happy to install a catheter, but at this point I am numb in a few select spots and raw in all the rest and quite sick of people tinkering with my genitals, even if they *are* trying to be helpful. Eventually, after a good cry and an embarrassingly long pep talk with myself, I manage to cough up the goods. Turns out my potty stint was time well spent; while I am in there I read the box of medicated witch hazel pads, which I discover I can use to line my diaper for the next several weeks. (Oh, come on! They told you that you'll need to wear a diaper for at least a month after giving birth, didn't they?) This nifty trick promises almost a full minute of cool, numbing relief for which I am eternally grateful.

7. Keep the baby's name a closely guarded secret until you fill out the birth certificate. This is partly to spare yourselves from hearing the endless catalog of negative associations that other people have with your unborn child's appellation (see the Trip Tip "Call It What You Will" following this chapter for details). The other reason to take a temporary vow of silence is that the minute you start bragging about the stunningly perfect name you've stumbled upon, it will get ripped off immediately. It's true. Brad and Angelina stole the name Pax from my friends Sharon and Ken before they could use it. We can't quite figure out *how* since the two families have never met, but Sharon swears she thought of it first, and she

isn't sure if she can ever forgive herself for not biting her tongue when she had the chance. And since there are approximately 193 countries in the world and Brangelina may, in fact, adopt a child from each of them, chances are *your* name will be snagged next if you let it slip. You really can't be too careful here.

8. It really doesn't matter what happens during those three or fifty-three hours it takes to bring your baby into the world. The second your child is born, it's all but forgotten—at least until the next time you encounter a pregnant woman. The only thing that matters the minute I look into my daughter's impossibly bright, clear eyes is that she is here, she is breathing, she has ten fingers and ten toes and a relatively normal-looking head, and she is mine. I survived delivery. I made a person. I've crossed the imaginary chasm that separates women from mothers, them from us. And as soon as the nurse brings me some ice, I'm having a margarita.

· ·

trip tip

Call It What You Will

THE BESTOWING OF A NAME upon your child is one of the most exciting, challenging and gut-wrenching parts of procreating. After all, the chosen moniker has to be something you won't tire of hearing (and let's face it, shouting) over and over (and over and over) for at least two decades; something you and your co-parent actually can agree on, something that's as unique as your child, but not so exceptional as to create a legacy of "Um, can you spell that?" in his or her endless future.

This might be a good time to point out what should be obvious: Hollywood is not reality, and unless you are a hotel heiress or rock royalty, going through life being named after a European capital city or popular produce item is probably not the ticket to popularity and happiness. (Imagine the pie references that poor Apple—fruit of the womb of actress Gwyneth Paltrow, of course—is going to have to deflect for the next decade, at least. Then picture confused little Reign Beau—bouncing bundle of Ving Rhames—at her first spelling bee. I mean, seriously. Have these people undergone a group lobotomy?)

No matter what names you are considering, I implore you to keep the list to yourselves, as there is not a handle in creation that someone, somewhere, will not find offensive. You think I'm crazy and paranoid? I may be a tiny bit of both (not to mention hypocritical), but believe me, even if you knock yourselves out to come up with something fabulous and meaningful, one of your nearest and dearest invariably once met a sleazy-looking stripper named Scarlett and another surely knew a shoe-chewing Rottweiler named Oliver, and even if you really, truly couldn't care less on a cellular level what "anyone else thinks," their comments will likely sting and might just lead you—in a fit of desperation—to the depths of parental despair where you give your child your own or your partner's name with "junior" slapped onto the end of it. (I beg you, don't. *Please.* "Jack! Jack Junior! Dinner is ready!" Ugh.)

Here's the rub: If you tell people you are *considering* a certain name, they'll drag it through the mud. (My sister-in-law actually said of a boy name we were considering: "We'll love him anyway." Fortunately we have a girl, whom we name Sophie Bella, which clearly is a flawless choice, but I'm still

trip tip

glad we kept it under wraps.) But even the most stalwart jerks will shut their traps once you introduce them to little Anita Taquito. Honest.

All of that being said, I encourage you to use this space to brainstorm, make notes and eventually—hopefully—come up with the perfect flag for your little fetus.

Names you like: _____

_____

_____

_____

Names your partner likes: _____

_____

_____

_____

Names you absolutely will not consider (can include exes, pets, unpopular family members, crooked congressmen, porn stars, finger foods, childhood bullies, feminine hygiene products, etc.): _____

_____

_____

_____

_____

Names you like but would sound hideous/silly/ridiculous with your last name (Kelly Green, Wanda Fonda, Mack Aroni, etc.): _____

_____

_____

_____

_____

Names you like but have the potential to be turned into unkind nicknames (this space intentionally large; remember, children are cruel. Little Martin is destined to be dubbed "Fartin' Martin" and Shelly will at least a handful of times be referred to as "Smelly Shelly," even if Martin isn't the least bit flatulent and Shelly is bathed twice daily): _____

_____

_____

_____

_____

Names you both agree on (this space left intentionally small for obvious reasons): _____

_____

IMPORTANT NOTE: It is wise to come up with a method of final selection, lest you find yourselves sending out announcements heralding the arrival of Baby Jones. My husband and I decided that the baby's sex would determine who got final say on the name. So while we both could have unlimited input, if it was a girl I got to name her (from a field of universally inoffensive choices), and if it was a boy he got to make the call. It worked for us—although I secretly feel that since it is the *woman* who has to forgo comfort, spicy foods, alcoholic beverages, slam-dancing and stomach-sleeping for ten months, she is absolutely entitled to fight for—and win— this privilege.

trip tip

7

I've Gotta Get
Out of This Place

I've been in this hospital for all of forty-eight hours, but it feels like forever. On the labor and delivery side, I was a pampered princess. Steamy, almost palatable food was delivered with delightful frequency, drugs were doled out like condoms on a college campus, nurses popped in just to say hello—one even offered a complimentary, unsolicited foot rub. My digs were spacious and cozy, and all of the unattractive, worrisome medical equipment was neatly sequestered behind soothing seafoam doors.

As soon as that baby plunges through the birth canal or abdominal incision, things change. Once you become a mom, the hospital apparently feels compelled to help you acclimate to your new life of austerity and sacrifice. Over here in the postpartum wing, my room is hardly bigger than my closet at home, the nurses border on surly, the food is inedible and the constant medical checks are exasperating. Poor Joe spends the night trying to fold his six-foot-three-inch frame into a doll-size, rock-hard pleatherette chair that the hospital generously refers to as a "cot." (Not.) I pine for a comfortable bed, edible food, a phone with voice mail and caller ID, and some clean, properly fitting underpants. More than anything, I'm dying to see how cute Sophie looks in her brand-spanking-new crib and exhaustive, lovingly pre-washed miniature wardrobe.

Joe inquires as to the discharge policies, and it seems I'm free to go seeing as I have produced the requisite bodily waste. As anxious as I am to leave, my gut response is *Really? I can leave? With the baby? You people don't even know where I live, or if I have any of the necessary supplies to care for her!* (Of course I have them all and more, but I could be homeless for all they know. I could be a homeless prostitute who keeps piranhas as pets. I mean, honestly. It's harder to adopt a stray dog than it is to acquire the rights to a human being!) I feel a combination of relief and panic.

I struggle back into the velour maternity sweat suit I wore into the joint, angrily eyeing the cute lounge set I brought and tried—with humiliating futility—to squeeze my engorged legs into. I cram it down into the depths of my overnight bag.

A nurse arrives with a wheelchair—a hospital policy I can't begin to fathom. One last teasing taste of the posh life before I become a slave to the greater procreative good? Or have I been such a royal pain in the ass here that they're not taking any chances that I might slip and fall on my way out the door and have to be readmitted?

"All set?" Joe asks.

Let's see: CD player we never turned on? Check. Ridiculously overpacked bag of unused toiletries and clothing that doesn't fit? Got it. Hundreds of dollars worth of overpriced, dying foliage? Present and accounted for. Stupid colossal rubber bouncy ball? "Sorry, nurse. Don't know *who* that belongs to. It was in the room when we got here." We have everything we came with—plus one implausibly tiny, slightly squirmy pink bundle I'm clutching to my chest tighter than a Midwestern tourist grips her purse on the New York City subway.

Down the hall, into the elevator, through the sweeping double doors and we're outside. It takes my eyes a few seconds to adjust to the blinding sunshine. The nurse waits with me while Joe runs to get the car. Even though it's a perfect spring day, the world suddenly seems like a big, mean, *dangerous* place.

"Hey, Mario Andretti! *Slow down!"* I shout as a truck barrels by. We're on a quiet little side street in a charming little town outside of a quaint little hospital, but it might as well be the Autobahn. I don't remember everyone on the road always being in such a hurry. The nurse just laughs.

Joe pulls up and I stand up on wobbly legs. Whether it's nerves, residual effects of the epidural or the fact that I've been on my back for two days is debatable. Probably a combination of the three. I open the back door and gently place Sophie into her top-rated, professionally installed, costs-half-as-much-as-the-car-itself car seat. *It's too big! Or she's too small!* Something isn't right. Even with the extra neck support roll we sprung for, she looks so tiny and fragile and helpless that I burst into tears. Her arms feel like brittle twigs beneath my trembling fingers, and I am genuinely afraid they might snap as I try to maneuver them underneath the straps of the AAA/AAP/CHP-approved five-point harness. Finally I get the thing snapped and pull the strap to make it just snug enough.

"Two fingers!" bellows the nurse, who is still standing there watching.

"Huh?" I say, spinning around and trying to wipe away my tears.

"You should only be able to get two fingers between the straps and her body." She practically pushes me out of her way and yanks the strap before I can stop her.

"That tight, really?" I gasp. Sophie lets out a wail and I have to bite the inside of my cheek to keep from joining her.

"No point in using it at all if you don't do it right," the nurse replies, giving me a condescending smirk.

I nod and climb into the front seat next to Joe, who puts the car into drive and starts inching away from the curb.

"You didn't even *look!*" I shout, a sound that startles Sophie. Now we're both crying.

"I *did* look, Jenna," he says calmly. Another half-block down the road, I can't take it.

"Pull over," I insist.

"Why?" he asks.

"Pull over!" I shout again, and before the car is even at a stop, I jump out the door, run around to the back and hop in next to Sophie. Joe shakes his head but says nothing. He inches along in appeasement, and I whisper soothing sounds at Sophie, my arms wrapped tightly around the bulk of her seat.

"Don't take the highway," I bark, ratcheting my grip another notch. "Take the back streets. And could you *slow down,* for heaven's sake?"

The two-mile drive to our house takes nine years (only a slight exaggeration). Finally we are home. I can't count the number of times I've fantasized about this moment. As Joe swings open the front gate—the gate I've gone through countless thousands of times alone—it occurs to me how weird it is that we left two days ago as two people, and now we're three. We're a *family.* I wonder how long it will take for this information to really sink in.

Inside I take Sophie to see her new room. Decorating it and assembling the army of fluffy stuffed animals, coordinating bedding and adorable artwork has been my guilty pleasure all these long months. She's frankly not impressed. The fact that babies can barely see past the tip of their noses (and in black and white, no less) seems immaterial. "You're going to love this room," I tell her, hoping I sound breezy and not at all like a martyr.

We pace around the house for a bit while I pretend to give her a little tour. I introduce her to the dog and the two cats plus her new bouncy seat, musical swing and activity mat before realizing that the term "new" is pretty relative here. I feel ridiculous. I'm not good at just...*being,* but I know I've got to try. I plop down on the couch and arrange her along my thighs so her tiny feet are pressing up against my not-so-tiny belly. Her arms flail about madly as if she's falling from a distant rooftop. I cup them gently and repeat the soothing *shhhhhhhh-shhhhhhhh-shhhhhhhh* mantra that I read can be particularly comforting, as it mimics the womb ambiance she grew to know and obviously love. Sweet heaven, it works. She quiets almost immediately and gazes up at me with the roundest, clearest eyes I've ever seen.

"You're an old soul, aren't you baby?" I whisper.

She gurgles up at me, and then a distinctive sound emanates from somewhere along my thighs.

"An old soul who needs a new diaper," Joe laughs.

The first diaper change in the new nursery! I'm actually excited. (This thrill gets old very quickly, so I suggest trying to enjoy the novelty while it's fresh.) I open the brand-new tube of diaper cream, pluck a fresh newborn diaper from the overstuffed diaper drawer and select a clean pair of pants. (Not that her tiny newborn poop is particularly stinky, but we *do* have all these clothes.) And of course, a new matching top. Again with the flimsy, floundering limbs! How does *any* baby make it to childhood and adolescence without breaking every single bone? I'm afraid to grip them too tightly, but she's surprisingly agile and I'll be here all night if I don't use a little muscle. I suddenly remember one of those forward-forward-forward e-mails I got a while back that offered a series of tests to help you determine whether or not you were ready to have a baby. One of the items suggested trying to stuff a large, angry octopus into a mesh bag. *Now* I see why that was so damned funny.

Finally she's dressed (and she looks positively smashing, even if no one appreciates this fact but me). I look at my watch and realize it's already time to feed her again.

"This is what we do now, Sophie," I tell my daughter—*I have a daughter!*—snuggling down in a big, soft chair.

She looks at me blankly, and who can blame her? I'm still not sure I believe it myself.

• •

trip tip

Is the Energizer Bunny the Devil in Disguise?

Children's toys and accessories share several similarities: They are frequently fashioned in a rainbow of décor-destroying primary colors; they often delight and amuse (children) by featuring a cacophony of competing sounds and songs, further enhanced by incessantly blinking, swirling, probing, pulsating, multicolored lights; and they always, without exception, require a minimum of four but sometimes as many as sixteen batteries.

Now, I'm not suggesting here that Fisher-Price is in bed with Duracell, but think about it: That bouncy seat/musical mobile/digital monitor is only as good as the 9-volts or double A's ramping it up. And while I can only vaguely recall the last time I changed the batteries in my hard-working TV remote (I think it was during a first-run episode of *Cheers*), something happens to those same little energy cells when you pop them into a child's toy: They last, on average, three hours. This has actually been scientifically proven—over and over—in my own home, so I know what I'm talking about here.

When the battery portion of your Costco bill begins to outweigh the foodstuffs, you will do what almost every rookie parent does at one time or another: You will invest hundreds of dollars into rechargeable batteries. This is a brilliant plan! Oh, wait. You forgot to buy the charger. (You might think it would make sense for this to come *with* the batteries, and you'd be right. But it doesn't.) Okay, now you're committed. The first time the batteries need charging, you will discover a slight flaw in the system. Since you have roughly 342 battery-requiring widgets on the premises, all of the other newfangled, chargeable batteries are currently in use. This means you will need an additional set of backups to use while the principal set is being re-juiced. No big deal; you go to Costco now every other day. The card-checker guy knows you by name. Another $150 (and a hot dog because they're only $1.50 and you get a *free drink!)* and you're set.

Until you discover this: Rechargeable batteries last about twenty-two minutes before they need charging again, and while it would *seem* simple enough to just plunk them into the charger, this rarely happens. Either you can't find it or it's not plugged in or you just don't want to deal with it, so you toss the batteries into a junk drawer. Months later you will pull them out and wonder *Why are these here? Are they still good?* And since going through the trouble of charging them just to find out they're worthless is out of the question, you will toss them (when no one is looking, of course, because you're pretty sure they contain toxic chemicals that ideally are disposed of by a hazmat team; also you *did* pay good money for them and there are starving people all over the world, and

trip tip

trip tip

even though you probably wouldn't have sent these folks a check if you *hadn't* bought the stupid batteries, somehow this seems wrong).

So now you're back to buying regular old disposable batteries, which is bleeding you dry financially and pushing you to the brink of madness. In children's toys, the insanity starts with the way batteries are housed—invariably behind a miniature door that fits into the toy only one way, which is impossible to get in or out through the very small Velcro slit in the toy's fur/fabric/outer shell, which is really irrelevant because there is absolutely no way to remove the eight Thumbelina-size screws holding the door in place once you get in there anyhow. Do they even make a screwdriver that small? But when your best mommy-friend lends you the tiny tool that came with her eyeglass-repair kit and you break in, you feel like you discovered where crop circles come from, figured out who killed King Tut and spotted Elvis, Nessie and Sasquatch all on the same day. You are Indiana Jones and that pesky Ark of the Covenant belongs to *you*!

Things rarely improve from here. You now discover that you need eight AAA batteries, even though you could have sworn the box said AA, so now you have to find a place to store the microscopic screws until your next Costco run. (This is where those otherwise useless "snack size" Ziploc bags come in handy.) Two days later, eight AAAs in hand, you must insert them into the compartment in a very precise fashion and in a specific—but never predictable—relationship to all of the others. Fortunately, there is usually a helpful diagram on the inside of the battery compartment detailing this divine placement. Unfortunately, the diagram is approximately the size of a single-celled protozoa, so good luck with that.

Eventually, out of sheer desperation, you start dropping them in there one at a time, willy-nilly. It shouldn't take more than a month or two to hit the proper sequence seeing as there are only sixteen thousand possible combinations. After three weeks with no food or sleep, you begin to suspect that the musical mobile/blinking play mat/vibrating rattle is a piece of crap and even if it isn't, it's definitely not worth your mental energy, so you chuck it into the trash. *Hard.* (This time you don't care who's looking. Enough is enough.) You will think you are losing your mind when you see and hear a strange blinking/flashing/giggling emanating from your trash can. *It's alive!* Without thinking you leap into the trash can with both feet and jump up and down until you have pummeled the offensive item into tiny, silent smithereens. Afterward, you fall onto the couch, thoroughly spent.

Almost immediately, you notice that your environment has assumed an unfamiliar but not altogether unpleasant air. You can't quite put your finger on it at first, but then you recognize it: Silence. Pure, peaceful, white, brilliant silence. Your living room no longer sounds, looks or feels like a Disney-themed discothèque. Even the thwack of a rubber mallet pounding a plastic workbench and the tumble of wooden blocks onto your bamboo floor sound like gentle breezes caressing a wind chime in comparison to the former racket.

At this point, you might be tempted to box up your collection of cordless crap and donate it to Goodwill. This is generous in theory, but in reality will only serve to perpetuate global frustration, which probably is not what the world needs right now. Trying to hawk the stuff on eBay or Craigslist or at your next garage sale is even worse because you would be profiting from another's pain and suffering.

trip tip

trip tip

Using these items to create a bonfire is another theoretical and enormously appealing solution, but possibly dangerous and/or illegal in your area (check your state's Department of Forestry and Fire Protection). I think the best solution is to mail the items—COD, of course—back to the manufacturer with a nice note. (Don't sign the note or include a return address. This adds to the mystery and fun!) Let them deal with landfill guilt. You're a parent now—you'll have enough guilt to last the rest of your life.

8

··

So *That's* What They're For!

I've wanted boobs all of my life, or at least for as long as I can remember. At one point, before my beloved friend Victoria began spilling her "secrets" (namely those marvelous, silicone gel-filled unmentionables I own in every shade and configuration), if a nearby friend ever found herself in a cotton-ball emergency, I might have been able to pluck one or two from my brassiere. I prayed for a growth spurt; slathered my torso with stinky creams; *I must, I must, I must* have performed ten thousand pushups and attempted half as many pull-ups—all in an effort to boost my nonexistent bust. Sure, when I was pregnant I got to bump up to a full B cup—sometimes the occasional vanity-sized C—although when your belly sticks out two feet in front of you and you weigh nearly as much as your brawny husband, this sort of gestational upsizing is almost irrelevant. In "real" life, my cups never did runneth over.

Be careful what you wish for.

I wake up five days postpartum soaking wet, in excruciating pain. I look frantically around me—is it blood? Sweat? Tears? The entire bed is drenched with clear, sweet-smelling liquid. *My water broke!* is my first fuzzy, frantic thought. Then I remember that, seeing as I already birthed the baby, that would be extremely worrisome, if not altogether impossible. I reach down in the near-dark to explore the source of the agony, but instead of the two smallish, downy mounds that used to reside above my rib cage, there stands a pair of impossibly taut beach balls that appear to have been maliciously overfilled with rocks. I hobble to the bathroom, my arms wrapped around my middle in an effort to buttress the Rockettes, which jut out a good six inches beyond my limbs. A trail of pearly droplets traces my path.

I literally scream when I see my reflection in the mirror: I look like a chubby, X-rated Jessica Rabbit. My once-humble, softly draping hooters are standing cadet-straight. These *mountainous* mounds look like two upturned gallons of vanilla ice cream drizzled with blueberry sauce and topped with fat slices of eggplant. Perhaps most distressingly, the freakish mammary feast is leaking like a cracked sewer pipe.

It's at this moment that I hear Sophie wake in the next room. "You're going to have to wait a sec, baby!" I shout with as much soothing nonchalance as I can muster. Then, to Joe: "Honey, can you try to distract her for a few minutes?" I realize I have given him an impossible assignment here, but I'm really left with no alternative. A hammerhead shark couldn't latch onto these things.

I jump into the shower, crank the handle all the way to the left and stand under the scalding spray. As gently as possible, I cup my monolithic triple D's and give them a soft squeeze. Milk shoots out in every direction. I admit to not paying much attention in anatomy class, but shouldn't I know that my own nipples have milk ducts on the *sides?* I genuinely do not recall digesting this bit of bodily trivia.

Even when I remove my hands, the Siamese geysers continue to erupt. The relief is indescribable.

Sophie's whimpers turn to wails and I know this is the new sound of duty calling. I give the twins one last firm tweak and pain shoots down into my toes and up into my earlobes. I actually shudder.

Not even bothering to stop and towel off, I bolt for the bed and Joe thrusts Sophie at me. Like an old pro, she latches on in record time. I'm lying on my side and she's snuggled against my front, and even though the breast she is not devouring is dripping right into her face, clearly she couldn't care less. Slowly, the pain—at least on the side in use—subsides and is replaced with an almost-pleasant-by-comparison prickling sensation. After a few minutes I dare to touch the side she is suckling and am amazed at how soft, supple and downright boulder-free it feels. She finishes the first course, I give her a quick burp and repeat the painful process on the other side, cursing myself for arrogantly refusing that complimentary can of formula they offered me in the hospital.

Alas, I come to discover, it won't be like this forever. This was just my milk "coming in." Whoever coined this little understatement might better have termed it "stampeding in." Charging, crashing, dashing, shooting, smashing or tearing in would work, too.

But pain, shmain! Nursing burns calories! Major calories. In fact, when you're pregnant, you only need a measly 250 extra of those villainous buggers a day *to create an entire person from scratch!* (So much for that whole "eating for two" business, unless the two in question are a pair of hummingbirds.) When you're breastfeeding, however, the additional calorie count skyrockets to a much more attractive five hundred. Never mind the fact that I am weak with hunger around the clock and could easily out-eat my 210-pound athlete husband at any all-you-can-eat buffet. That's ten guilt-free Oreos a day. Three monster meatballs dripping in marinara sauce. Half of a grilled double-decker club sandwich. An entire cup of Ben and Jerry's Chunky Monkey. No wonder some women are still nursing their eight-year-olds. Beats the heck out of a two-hour kickboxing class.

Newborn babies, you might be interested to know, nurse anywhere from eight to sixteen times a day. On the high end of that scale, at twenty minutes per side per feeding, with five minutes between sides for a good burping, you're looking at doing absolutely nothing—not even squeezing in a quick pee unless you're nursing on the john—for 720 minutes (that's *twelve solid hours* every day) except feeding your baby. Just nursing around the clock. The upside to the high end is that at least you don't have to worry about what to do with all of your frustrating free time.

At Sophie's two-week pediatric checkup, I develop a newfound respect for my body's propensity for producing food that goes far beyond its ability to burn fat and kill time. Sophie has gained sixteen whole ounces since birth—all of which came straight from my body. I congratulate her heartily, knowing this may well be the last time in my little girl's life that she will be praised for packing on a pound.

I quickly learn that any time I go beyond, say, two hours between feedings, the rocks return, sometimes with a vengeance similar to their debut. I've read some books that advocate nursing on demand, and others that praise the scheduled-feeding method. I'm a little torn. On one hand, as a self-confessed control freak, the idea of knowing roughly when the booby buffet will be open is immensely appealing. On the other hand, it seems pretty cruel (if not out of the question) to deprive a tiny, rumbling tummy.

Eventually I decide on a combination of the two methods. What this means is I won't wake her to eat, as some of the books suggest (except for the rocks, it's pretty easy to get behind the "never wake a sleeping baby" philosophy), even if doing so happens to throw the precious schedule off kilter. But if she wakes and can be distracted until the two-hour mark, I'll go that route.

One of my parenting books informs me that babies have seven different cries, one each for hunger, temperature-related discomfort, fear, fatigue, sickness, confusion and one (not the author's words) essentially for when they're pissed off for no good reason. This book goes on to say—honest to God—that parents can learn to distinguish these wailings. Right now they all sound identical to me. If hard-pressed, I'd say they fall into the by-and-large-pissed-off category. Who can blame her? If I were in a strange place filled with unfamiliar sounds and smells, I didn't speak the native language, my stomach were the size of a peanut—and someone cruelly put me on an all-liquid diet when, thus far, food had always been deposited conveniently into my belly—and I'd never in my entire life had a "good night's sleep," I'd be mighty ornery, too.

The feeding plan seems to be working. Frequently I am able to easily and guiltlessly distract Sophie until the appointed eating time. When I can't, she gets the boob. No big deal. I begin to feel the stirrings of confidence. I can do this!

One day, Sophie starts crying shortly after I finish feeding her. She's probably not hungry, I reason, so I decide to try out my sleuthing skills. She doesn't look particularly angry. Or confused. And her skin doesn't feel warm or clammy. Could her cry have a hint of an "I'm tired" pitch to it? Even though she's only been up for forty-five minutes, I lay her down in her bassinette to test my instincts. She immediately falls asleep. Two minutes later, I flop down on the bed next to her, exhausted. The phone rings almost at once.

"Whatcha doing?" Joe asks by way of a greeting.

"I just finished working out and Sophie's asleep," I whisper, employing our new codeword for nursing.

"Good for you," he says, laughing. "Why don't you go take a nap yourself?"

At least I *think* that's what he says. A half hour later I wake to the sounds of an unmistakable "feed-me" wail.

The (slumber) party's over, at least for now.

9

Pay at the Pump

In more than one awe-inspiring video shown in Prenatal Prep, we watched as a newborn babe wormed its way up its new mom's belly and located its intended food source. By sheer instinct and fundamental need, these intrepid creatures were able to engage in the act of nursing that is one of nature's most beautiful and profound.

Pumping breast milk, on the other hand, is about as organic and intuitive as watching a monster truck rally on TV while downing a bag of Doritos.

The impetus for engaging in this perverted practice is to stockpile milk in the event you will be separated from your babe, whether for planned or unplanned reasons. Plus, the prevailing wisdom goes, pumping helps stabilize your milk supply (I foolishly thought this was the baby's job). Finally, having an extra stash of milk allows partners, babysitters and other family members the privilege of participating in the joys of feeding. Since I have the distinct luxury of working from home when I do resume working, and since I have no immediate plans to take off on a solo stint across South America, I don't anticipate a high demand for this substitute food supply. Nevertheless, I spring for the Mercedes of breast pumps, the Medela Pump in Style, because if I'm going to engage in this bizarre ritual, I definitely want to do it "in style."

Another bit of questionable logic suggests that having bottled breast milk on hand allows mom to get some much-needed rest while dad (or her "parenting partner," or whatever the PC term is these days for the may-or-may-not-be-related person of undetermined gender who is equally responsible for the baby) takes over a feeding or two. What this theory fails to address is the fact that mom's body doesn't get the memo to *not produce milk* during the sudden window of proposed sleep, so she's awake in dripping discomfort anyway. Does it make any sense whatsoever to artificially drain your breasts with an unloving appliance while your tot grudgingly suckles a bottle in the next room? Sure, you have another bottle of liquid gold when you're done, in most cases exactly the amount that the baby just downed. I'm no math whiz, but it's pretty clear that the net result is a big, fat zero. Once again, I question the sanity of the people who are coming up with these parenting theories.

Still, I do it. At least, I try (because I could get hit by a truck or struck by lightning, and never mind the fact that I, along with millions of other semi-normal people on the planet, was given nothing but formula as an infant, my child is getting the real deal if it kills me—which, at this moment, I suspect it just might.)

The maiden voyage is terrifying. I sequester myself in my abandoned office and assemble the various pump parts, eyeing the funnel-shaped vacuum attachments with great suspicion. I place one of the cones over one of my breasts and hold it there while I use the other hand to turn the machine on. There are five settings to choose from, so I start at one, the lowest. The machine makes a strange gurgling sound, but I don't feel any sort of tug from the funnel. Gingerly I take the other funnel and begin moving it toward my other breast. When it comes within an inch of my flesh, the funnel seems to leap out of my hand and latch onto my nipple with the force of one of those high-end European vacuum cleaners. I watch in horror as it draws my nipple out until it is approximately eight feet long. Much like those labor contractions, it slowly subsides, only to be replaced by an identical drag on the other side. I desperately want to turn the machine down (which is not an option) or off, but I'm afraid if I let go of the funnels my breast tissue will get completely sucked into the motor.

I watch this horror show for a good three or four minutes, but nothing seems to be happening. Finally, tiny banana-yellow droplets of syrupy goo begin appearing on the necks of the funnels. They don't seem to be accumulating into anything resembling the milk I am hoping will fill the bottles attached to the torturous contraption, but at least it's something.

For twenty minutes I sit and patiently allow my body to be suckled by a machine. At the end of this interminable period, I am rewarded with a whopping four ounces of milk, three of which disconcertingly come from one boob.

"Almost everyone has an overproducer and an underproducer," my sister informs me. In my case, she's dead right. Every time I pump, I get the 3-to-1 ratio, with the bulk consistently coming from the same enthusiastic side. We nickname my breasts "over" and "under," and I'm relieved to know that this is normal (the uneven production, not necessarily the naming of one's mammaries).

As time passes, pumping becomes more comfortable and I manage to work my way up to the higher settings. Eventually, it gets to the point where I can flip the switch to setting five, plunk the funnels down simultaneously and even use my other hand to peruse the latest Pottery Barn catalog while the thing does its job.

I manage to amass a decent store of milk, but it never feels like enough. It all goes into the freezer, because the guidelines for how long breast milk stays fresh in the refrigerator are wildly inconsistent (anywhere from six hours to eight days), and it's really only there for emergencies. Even in the freezer, if you use a frequently opened double-door model, you're looking at a shelf life of three months, max (six months if you have a drop-in freezer used exclusively for this purpose and keep the temperature set below zero degrees—which, doesn't everyone?).

When the handwritten expiration dates on my meager bags of frozen milk begin to close in, my anxiety escalates. Throwing one out is harder than burying a beloved family pet. I have to face the fact that you really can only get so much blood—or in this case, milk—from a stone. If I perish tomorrow, the frozen stash might last two weeks. Sophie would still need several months of formula before she could switch over to regular cow's milk (which, once you've milked your own body, doesn't seem so regular after all). But since "anything is better than nothing," I forge on, somewhat unenthusiastically.

At one point, I notice something strange. The repetitive whoosh-pull of the pump's motor seems to sound like a word, or several words. It's hard to make out at first, but then I hear it with crystal clarity: "Puuuuuuuuuuuump-ing, puuuuuuuuuuuuuuuump-ing, puuuuuuuuuuuuuump-ing," it says, over and over. Like the famous Little Engine, my thoughtful, encouraging mechanical friend is telling itself—and me—that we can do this!

I have heard about women who go off the deep end after delivery, so I mention this to my friend Pam. "Oh, my pump talked to me, too," she says matter-of-factly.

"Did it say 'puuuuuuuuuuuump-ing' over and over?" I ask eagerly.

"No, mine said, 'Be careful,'" she insists.

I look at my machine fondly, glad I didn't accidentally buy the Pump in Angst model. That's the last thing I need right now.

●●

trip tip

Midnight in the Garden of . . . Pure Evil

FEEDING A BABY at ungodly hours of the day and night is an activity fraught with peril. Some of the booby traps, if you will, are well known and oft discussed. Sore nipples? Get a gallon of lanolin cream, apply regularly and go topless as often as possible or convenient. Shelf life of formula? Best-by date is right there on the canister. Baby is fussy and squirmy after only a half-feeding? Burp her, rub her back or bicycle her legs...and wait.

But here's a little something no one talks about: the havoc this downtime can wreak on your financial health. See, there will be long stretches, often in the wee hours of the night, during which—unless you have a massively stocked TiVo lineup, an extensive collection of educational DVDs or a friend in Australia who might be awake concurrently—you will be forced to watch whatever is on the tube at the time. And pretty much all you'll find on TV in the middle of the night are infomercials. If you haven't channel-surfed at 2:00 a.m. recently, you may be blissfully unaware of the arsenal of gadgets, gizmos and gazillionaires-hawking-how-to-get-rich-buying-foreclosed-properties-schemes there are in the world today, all of them available for just six easy payments of $149.99, plus shipping and handling. Did you know they make super-slimming coffee (regular and decaf)? Yup, you just drink the stuff and the fat melts right off. Really.

trip tip

And how come *Better Sex Through Yoga* isn't a health-club staple yet? If you're doing yoga anyhow, who wouldn't enjoy this little perk? There's even a handy gadget out there that heats hot dogs and buns at the same time. I mean, that nuisance has been plaguing gourmands for decades! And to think, the joys and virtues of all of these items have been repeatedly extolled, night after night, while you had the audacity to sleep. Fortunately, those days are over!

During one particularly endless stint manning the midnight buffet, I actually buy—and I have the receipt to prove it—the Scunci Steamer, "the world's finest lightweight pressurized steamer, specially designed to easily clean and sanitize nearly everything in and around your home without the use of chemicals." Now, I ask you: Do you think the marketing team behind this product accidentally chose this time slot to hawk it? Or bought it simply because it was cheap? Of course not! They know that exhausted, insecure, germ-phobic moms (okay, and maybe a few neat-freak drunks) will be glued to their couches, unable to resist the prospect of a naturally clean home.

Before I can even find a spare minute to open the Steamer and discover it is a certified piece of crap, my new Seal-a-Meal Vacuum Food Keeper (with Microban Antimicrobial Protection!) arrives. Hot on its heels is *Rich Dad, Poor Dad,* the audio series. That one happens to arrive the same day as a rather alarming Visa bill, so this Poor Mom promptly returns it, unopened, to Mr. Kiyosaki, with only a tinge of guilt for reducing his hard-earned Passive Income by three figures.

I am not lying to you, I swear. I actually buy these items. I am *this close* to ordering the Time/Life multi-disc collection *Superhits of the '60s, '70s and '80s,* but I forget the toll-free number before I can find the phone. I should add here that Joe bought me an iPod for Christmas last year, so CDs are mostly obsolete in our house. When I confess these purchases to my sister, she admits to milking-and-buying a few times. (The woman bought a ThighMaster, for crying out loud! Like any new mom needs *that* staring at her from the corner of the living room.)

All of this is simply to say: Don't buy anything you see on TV. Ever. But especially not in the middle of the night. And whatever you do, don't get sucked in by those "order in the next five minutes and we'll slash a payment!" lies. Do you think the phone operators sitting out in a windowless call center in Hoboken are staring at their watches, waiting for the "golden opportunity" moment to pass? The price is the price and always will be the price, and no matter how many payments they break it down into or offer to cut, it's still too much.

Whenever you get the urge to spit out your credit card number, use these pages to make notes about enticing potential shopportunities. After careful consideration, Google your cordless can opener/invisible tummy trimmer/ergonomic ice cream scoop, check Epinions or BizRate for reviews, ask your friends if they own or have ever heard of the particular must-have, life-altering widget you are obsessing over. Then, and only then, if you still think it's a sound investment, wait a week to prove to yourself it is not an impulse purchase, and then try to find your Fantabulous BugVac on eBay first. Hint: If there are dozens of them being offered for obscenely low "buy it now" prices, there is probably a good reason.

trip tip

trip tip

Crap I am almost positive I need but probably don't:

_____

_____

_____

_____

_____

_____

_____

_____

_____

_____

_____

_____

_____

_____

_____

Can I Get Some
Help Around Here?

There was a time in my life when I wore high heels and went to parties. Sometimes I even wore high heels *to* parties if precarious footwear was appropriate; I still have a closet full of strappy stiletto sandals to prove it. At the moment they're cowering beneath an army of hiphugger pants, sleeveless body-skimming tops and impossibly clingy dresses that look, in terms relative to my current body size and shape, as if they belong to a 13-year-old girl. Facing these vestiges of my less-corpulent self is more depressing than any Meryl Streep movie, so I box up the whole mess and stuff it in my office closet until further notice. The remaining three pairs of elastic-waist maternity pants and half-dozen muumuus look lonely hanging there, but I refuse to invest in a wardrobe of companions for them out of the vain hope that I will be skinnying into my old clothes any day now.

By one month postpartum, I've lost a whopping twelve pounds, nearly nine of which were pure baby. I still have thirty-five more than I started this adventure with—minus the fashionable bump. I notice that most of these unwanted fat cells have found homes in my thighs, my arms, beneath my bra strap (the dreaded "back fat") and in a bizarre shelf-like position below my waist and above my hipbones that can only be described as haunches. (My friend Darrell informs me that the technical term for these is "muffin tops." I briefly resent her for enlightening me.) Apparently a handful of these blubber pockets have even decided that my chin affords some lovely views and have set up camp there. If I were stranded in my car in a snowstorm today, I'd have enough junk in my bodily trunk to keep me warm for several weeks.

As long as I am toting Sophie around, I don't mind the excess flab as much as I would have thought. (A baby makes a great accessory and, if carried strategically in a front pack, hides a multitude of lumps.) But on the rare occasions I get out of the house solo, usually to run to the grocery store for a fresh stockpile of wipes or a new tube of nipple cream, I refuse to make eye contact with anyone out of fear that they might ask me when I am due—or the equally crippling dread that they won't. I fantasize about designing a line of "transition tees" with quippy sayings like "temporarily tubby" and "recently made a person," but forming a start-up company would probably take more time and energy than a good tooth-brushing, and I can barely manage *that* these days.

Before long it occurs to me that no one is looking at me anyway. This is a bittersweet pill to swallow. You see, I'd gotten used to being the center of attention. At any given moment while I was expecting, friends, acquaintances and perfect strangers were interested in my every endeavor. How was I feeling, sleeping, eating, they wanted to know. Now that there's a tiny, helpless, strangely bald-yet-furry creature wearing an impossibly cute sequin-cherry knit cap in the room, I could have flames shooting out of my ears and no one would notice. It's *The Sophie Show* now and I have a feeling I'd better get used to it.

The good news is that I am as smitten with her as the rest of the world appears to be. I am familiar with Brooke Shields's tragic tale and have several friends who suffered from various degrees of postpartum depression, so I am happy to report feeling mostly unscathed in that arena. While I do experience moments of hopelessness (usually surrounding the subject of sleep and the question of whether I'll ever get any again), I am pleasantly surprised to discover that I seem to possess some maternal instincts after all. I can spend hours just staring at my daughter, and when Joe asks later what we did today, I honestly cannot answer. I take dozens of pictures and send out hard drive-clogging e-mail files almost daily with no discrimination whatsoever. Never mind that every photo looks identical, being that she is a blob and doesn't do all that much. She is perfect and beautiful and I must catalogue her every yawn and (more importantly) every outfit.

I nurse, we walk, I rock, we sing songs, I take more pictures and even the occasional shower. Finally, she smiles. *There's a person in there! I can go on!* Shortly afterward, she is lying prone and pushing up with her tiny little arms when she accidentally rolls over. *The person can learn tricks!* One day, I think I even spot the beginnings of a tooth coming in, but it turns out to be thrush.

The weeks begin to pass in a blur. It's not that time is moving faster than usual, it's simply that every day is exactly the same and therefore indistinguishable from the previous one. I start to feel antsy. Day after day we bounce and bond and I wonder if other new moms feel as isolated as I do. During Sophie's naps, I shuffle around the house, organize drawers and occasionally make small talk with the FedEx guy. I am still head over heels in love with my baby—it's Joe I'm beginning to hate.

"Goodbye girls!" he announces cheerfully every morning, briefcase in hand, loyal Labrador by his side. "Off to the trenches!"

"Bye Daddy," we mutter back. Why is it that my life has changed so drastically and Joe's hasn't? What would it be like to come and go as I pleased again? How could I have taken such an indulgence for granted? I can't even remember what that kind of freedom feels like.

What's wrong with me? I wonder. This is supposed to be the most fulfilling job on Earth! There's no question that I would throw myself in front of a delivery truck for my baby, and she is arguably the sweetest, most striking clump of cells ever assembled. Even her poop has a delightful, buttered-popcorn aroma. But the monotony is becoming unbearable. I need to have an adult conversation (with someone other than my husband) that lasts longer than forty-five seconds and doesn't contain the words "gas" or "hind milk." If this doesn't happen soon, I am pretty sure my head will explode.

I try getting back to work. Seeing as I write from home, I have the luxury of working around Sophie's schedule. I'll just write when she's sleeping, I think foolishly. Of course, that's also when I'm supposed to be doing laundry and cleaning and cooking and penning thank-you notes and rearranging the pantry and catching up on all the sleep I'm not getting at night. Alas, not much actual writing ensues.

"We need a babysitter," I tell Joe.

"So hire one," he replies.

This isn't the first time it occurs to me that somehow, unwittingly, I have assumed the role of Default Caregiver. Time for Sophie's latest round of shots? I make the appointment. Sophie's got a fever? I decide whether to give her Motrin or Tylenol or sit with her in the steamy bathroom or take her to the pediatrician or do nothing at all. It's not that Joe is incapable of snipping her microscopic fingernails with the doll-sized clippers or wielding a thermometer—but he's made it clear that where Sophie is concerned, I can ask him to do virtually any task, but I cannot tell him how to do it. Since silent acquiescence isn't in my repertoire, I wind up doing most of the mundane stuff myself.

So I set out to find some part-time help. Our parent-friends swear by the infamous local Brazilian babysitting ring, so I schedule a few interviews. By the fourth one, I realize why they didn't name the movie *Blame It on Bakersfield*. I've never been to Brazil, so I'm not sure if all of the women there are drop-dead gorgeous or if they simply ship the most stunning of the bunch over here. I am so sleep-deprived I actually think maybe I mistakenly said I was looking for a Playmate and not a *play mate.* Call me shallow, but I refuse to intentionally invite thirteen miles of toned, tanned legs into my house, even if they *are* willing to fold my laundry and empty the Diaper Genie.

Once I weed through and promptly dismiss all of the mannequins, I put help-wanted ads in the paper and on Craigslist. *Part-time babysitter needed. Must have experiences and references. Salary negotiable.*

It doesn't take long to discover that the candidate pool is dismally shallow. The first respondent is forty-five minutes late, which would be enough to send her immediately packing, but the dingbat actually locks her keys in her car, so I am stuck making small talk while we wait for AAA (my account) to come bail her out. Next, there's Stinky Gal, who apparently thinks a bottle of musky perfume overrides the cigarette stench she's clearly trying to mask. After her comes the original Valley Girl ("Like, omigod, I totally *love* kids and I want to have a million but not yet or anything 'cuz, you know, my boyfriend doesn't even have a job and I am, like, totally not even ready for that kind of responsibility."). Just when I think I've seen everything, You Can't Be Serious Chick pulls up—in a shiny new Range Rover. "I charge $22 an hour including drive time, and I need full health insurance," she informs me. "And I don't change diapers." I wonder if she couldn't get a job at Starbucks because she "doesn't make coffee." I daydream about getting in my car and driving away, maybe just for a cruise up the coast or even a whole weekend alone, something I would never do, even though the idea is immensely appealing.

Finally, hope appears on my doorstep like a sliver of sunshine after a month of torrential rain. Sarah is soft and girl-next-door pretty and says "Hey" in a sweet Southern twang when I open the door. *What's wrong with her*, I wonder, clearly jaded by this point. Is she a thief? A homewrecker? A kidnapper? A gun-toting bunny-boiler? Sarah reaches out and lifts Sophie from my arms, and in that instant she could be wearing a Freddy Kruger mask and I might decide she's just got a silly sense of humor. Sophie looks up at her and gurgles, and Sarah seems to melt before my eyes. The two of them are cooing and smiling adoringly at one another and I am standing there as if I don't exist anymore, and I'm not even jealous because I need a break so badly I can taste it.

"When can you start?" I demand, temporarily unconcerned about her ethics or work history or driving record or potential criminal past.

"Right away?" she drawls, and it's all I can do not to kiss her smack on the lips. She's my salvation and I'm not going to do anything to scare her away.

* * *

trip tip

Hiring a Hand to Rock the Cradle

YOU MAY FIRMLY BELIEVE that the only person qualified to care for your child is one who is directly responsible for his or her genetic profile. If that is your stance, I respect and applaud you and wish you endless rewarding years of uninterrupted, round-the-clock quality time with your offspring. However, there *may* come a time—you have a proctologist appointment, your best friend gets arrested and you need to bail her out of jail, your partner is away on a business trip and you get invited to a Tupperware party—when you need an hour or seven of child-free time. This is, of course, just a vague possibility. But should it occur, rather than scrambling for last-minute help (everyone has caller ID these days, and trust me, no one answers when they see the name of a new parent flashing across the screen), it's wise to be prepared. *Just in case.*

If money is no object, feel free to start with a high-priced nanny service and interview nothing but their arsenal of thoroughly prescreened and overqualified applicants. You can also take out your own ad in the local paper, post one at a local college or on their web site, or try advertising on a job site like Craigslist or Monster. Here's a sample ad you might want to consider:

Loving, Responsible Babysitter Wanted

Hi! We are looking for an experienced, honest person to care for our easygoing _____-month-old _____ (boy/girl/twins/triplets/quads). Qualified candidate must be prompt, courteous and flexible, and have a clean driving record. References a must; pay commensurate with experience. If interested, please call at your earliest convenience—we look forward to meeting you! (Your phone number here.)

TRANSLATION: Hi! (Exclamation points convey friendliness and lack of desperation!) We are looking for an experienced (you *have* done this before, right?), honest (don't steal our stuff because we have expensive hidden cameras everywhere and will prosecute to the fullest extent of the law) person (although I don't think you can, by PC-law, specify "woman," be careful here. I have scheduled interviews via e-mail with Chris, Aaren and Kim—all of whom turned out to be men. Now, I am aware of the "manny" trend, and you are welcome to call me sexist, but I cannot for the life of me discern a respectable reason why a twenty-two-year-old male would want to spend long hours with a two-month-old girl) to care for our easygoing

(cross your fingers when you type this) _____-month-old _____ (boy/girl/twins/triplets/quads). Qualified candidate must be prompt (this is vital; you can't imagine how eager to get out that door you might be), courteous (no dirty looks when I'm chatting on the phone, and *no chatting on the phone)* and flexible (i.e., willing to come early/stay late/unload the dishwasher/help me into my girdle/take a check written out in crayon), and have a clean driving record (everyone says this, although I'm not quite sure it's vital if you don't plan to have the sitter driving the baby around—except it makes you look conscientious). References a must (check these if you feel compelled, but it's not like she's going to give you the name/ number of the family whose plasma TV she lifted or kid she abandoned to run out for a fresh pack of smokes); pay commensurate with experience (If you've done this before, you can name your price). If interested, please call at your earliest convenience—we look forward to meeting you! (You have NO idea how badly. But I'm not desperate, really.) (Your phone number here.) (Never, ever, put your home phone number in this ad. Applicants will call at the very moment the kitchen timer is going off and the frozen lasagna drippings are burning all over the oven floor, setting off the smoke alarm, and the dog is barking at the UPS guy who is repeatedly ringing the bell and shouting "I need a signature, ma'am!" through the door, and the baby in question is (understandably) screaming bloody murder and the person you are hoping will take you away from all of this will hang up before you even get to the "o" in "hello." ALWAYS give your cell number, and only take calls when the baby is asleep, the dog is outside, the oven is turned off and Enya is playing softly in the background.)

**When meeting applicants in person,
keep this list of questions handy for the interview:**

So, can you tell me a little bit about yourself? Seems obvious, but this is a good chance to see if the candidate can follow simple directions you may later give her, such as "Do not answer the door when I am gone or put bourbon in the baby's bottle." You asked for a *little bit.* Does she share her entire life story? Go on and on about her boyfriend's band/Doberman's skin condition/roommate's eating disorder? What you want to hear is something like this: "I'm the oldest of six children and have always loved being around kids. I was a youth counselor at my church for three summers, I've been babysitting since I was eleven and I volunteer at the Boys & Girls Club whenever I have time. Also I'm terribly neat and love doing dishes." Again, this is just a suggested dream-reply. Use your good judgment.

What do you enjoy most about working with babies/ children? Obviously she's not going to say, "Oh, probably changing poopy diapers and washing puke out of my hair," and if she does, escort her promptly to the door as she is a suck-up, a pathological liar, a wacko or all three. Still, if she hems and haws and can't spit out something reasonable about thriving in the presence of innocence and the euphoric feeling she gets from the sweet smell of baby powder, she's clearly just in it for the free Cheetos. *Next.*

How do you deal with frustration? This is a trick question, because you want her to say, "Oh, I never get frustrated!" You see, babies are frustrating! Alas, as long as she doesn't say,

"I bang my head on the wall/snort something illegal/take a long drive by myself…" she's probably fine.

Are you CPR/first-aid certified? Never mind that you aren't; she should be. It shows initiative and, well, could be a life-saver, literally. End of discussion.

What's your typical hourly rate? If she aced all of the above questions, this is irrelevant. Pay her whatever she asks for and do it with a smile.

This is not a question, but something to observe: How big are her breasts? No, really. This is important. You probably think I'm going to suggest you avoid bringing a statuesque glamazon into your home at the very moment when you are feeling…well, less than glamorous. That is where you would be dead wrong. Here's the thing: My husband—an amazingly astute fellow—noticed early on that every single female who responded to our babysitter ad was more than a little over-endowed in the mammary department. Their body types were all over the map—short, tall, Rubenesque, rail-thin, athletic, couch potato—and it mattered not; their fronts all sported an alarming pair of five-gallon jugs. His theory: A woman's bra size is directly related to her maternal capacity (if he's right, I'm in dire trouble, although perhaps this is only critical in women who choose to watch someone *else's* child in exchange for money). I doubted this theory until I once "borrowed" a flat-chested sitter from a friend in an emergency. Becca turned out to be colder than a frozen fishsicle and only slightly less engaging. Now I, too, am a believer, but I encourage you to test the theory for yourself and report back with your findings!

II

....

Your Baby Is Cute, Too—But Can She Spell "Pretentious"?

Once the magnificent Sarah starts babysitting, my spirits lift almost immediately. Just having another person around the house a few hours a week who can sit up unassisted is refreshing. Even though I eventually do ask for (and actually check) Sarah's references, for several weeks I find excuses to stay home every time she babysits. I make a great production of going up to my office to work and doubt she ever suspects I'm spying on her interactions with Sophie through the baby monitor. (If they called it a "babysitter monitor" I am sure some civil rights group would protest, even though I have since confirmed that most of my friends have used these gizmos to execute similar recon missions.)

No matter how often or long I listen in, Sarah is endlessly patient and terrifically loving, and I find myself thinking more than once that she might just turn out to be a better caregiver than I am. Eventually I have enough faith—and sufficient experiential evidence that she will not abandon my child to run outside and fire up a joint the minute I turn my back—to actually leave the house.

The first time I venture out for some precious me-time, I feel like Ellie May Clampett discovering Rodeo Drive. Were there always so many fabulous things to ogle in the stores—and were they always this expensive? Have there always been this many cars on the road? Was everyone in the world always so thin and put-together? And when did velour hoodies go out of style? I've been out with Sophie a few times, but on each of those excursions I was so focused on not dropping, losing or forgetting her or her arsenal of accessories that I was oblivious to the world around me. I find it exhilarating and depressing at the same time.

I call home to check in no fewer than six times an hour. *Is she still sleeping? Did you check to make sure she's breathing? Well, check! But don't wake her up. You know where the laminated CPR instruction card is, right? And the fire extinguisher? I'm five minutes away, so call me if you have any questions. But if it's an emergency, call 911 first. Nine-one-one, you got that, right? Maybe you should program it into your phone. Do you want me to come home and do it for you?*

Like anything, the more I get out, the easier it becomes. Maybe we should find a playgroup, I think. You know, mix it up a bit. I tell myself that Sophie needs the socialization, but the truth is she'd be perfectly content to sit in her pint-size vibrating Barcalounger and bat aimlessly at the blinking shapes that hang above her head all day, every day. It's me who needs the outside human contact and change of scenery.

I have no shortage of wonderful friends, but something happens when you join the Parents' Club. None of my mommy-friends told me about it (and now I understand why), and my not-yet or not-ever mommy friends, like me, obviously weren't in the know. You have to have a baby of your very own before you realize that moms don't just want to hang out with other moms, they want to hang out with moms who have kids the exact same age and preferably the same sex as their kids (although the gender part can be negotiable, especially early on).

Most important of all, they want to hang out with moms who share identical parenting styles and philosophies. On-demand or scheduled? Extinction or attachment? Cow's milk or soy? Cloth or disposable? Homemade or store-bought? Pharmaceutical or herbal? Firm, loving discipline or tantrum-throwing nightmare? Meeting someone who mirrors your idealism *that you actually like* may be harder than finding decent-looking designer shoes in your size at Nordstrom Rack.

I locate a mommy-and-me group and sign up feeling cautiously optimistic. We arrive at the first meeting to find a room packed with sixty-plus women and seventy-plus babies (a few of these intrepid souls have birthed twins and even triplets, God bless their weary souls). I am immediately overwhelmed. Not only is there not even a single familiar face in the crowd, but the room is stiflingly hot and smells as if every last one of the darling little tikes in attendance needs an urgent diaper change.

Nevertheless, I take a seat, because where else am I going? We're dressed, we're out of the house and the prospect of another endless carbon-copy day at home is unbearable. We sit in a gigantic circle and make polite chitchat with our neighbors as each new mom waits for her turn to stand and report on the week's high and low moments. I'm contemplating my low—was it when Sophie pooped in her car seat from her ankles to her armpits and I had just used my last diaper, or was it when I actually managed to find the time to whip up a casserole for dinner and proceeded to drop the bubbling beauty on the floor—when I catch the strains of a nearby conversation.

"Is Becca rolling over yet?" Tyler's mom asks the woman next to her. Tyler, you see, has been rolling over since he was two months old, the little rascal.

"Um, not really, no," replies Becca's flustered mom. Poor Becca is a bit of a runt and never mind the fact that she was born three whole weeks after Tyler; now Becca's mom is positive there is something fundamentally wrong with her and will inevitably dash home and schedule a pricey home visit with the hoity-toity developmental specialist.

"I've been reading little Lorna the classics since before she was born," brags a mineral water-sipping snob with a Louis Vuitton diaper bag. I take an immediate dislike to her.

"Lexus loves the Baby Einstein flashcards," chimes in another pompous parent. "I think she really has a gift for appreciating art."

"Really?" I jump in, even though Lexus's and Lorna's moms are clearly enjoying their game of one-upwomanship without any insight or input from me. "That's great! Sophie seems to like *The Sopranos,* so we watch that a lot. We have every episode on DVD." This is not true, of course. I don't even like TV and I've never seen *The Sopranos.* But I know it's extremely violent and I can't help it, I want to shut these women up. I realize I'm digging my own grave, but if my choices are Olympic Compare-a-thoning or a lifetime of solitary confinement, I'll pad the cell myself.

"You just got the wrong group!" my friend Tami insists when I call her later to complain. Tami has a four-year-old and twin toddlers— all boys—and still meets weekly with the mommy group she fell into immediately after her oldest son was born.

"There were more than sixty women there!" I cry. "Practically every woman who's given birth in this town in the past six months belongs to that group and I couldn't stand a single one of them!"

"Jenna, try again," she implores. "You don't know how much you need this."

"Did you join a new group with the twins?" I ask her.

"Oh God, of course not!" she laughs. "And sit around and listen to a bunch of women complain about how hard it is to have *one* baby?"

I feel like a shmuck for even asking, so I promise her I'll try it again. Instead, I have a lightbulb moment and e-mail my prenatal group to see if anyone is interested in a reunion. Maybe we didn't agree on pregnancy protocol, but perhaps now that we're all toting newborns we'll have something in common. Apparently I'm not the only one jonesing for adult company because every last one e-mails back to say she'll be at the first get-together at my house the next week.

Our soiree is somewhat awkward at first because we really don't know each other all that well, apart from the fact that we're pretty sure we all were getting lucky at about the same time last year and we could all use a little undereye concealer.

We sip lemonade and nibble on scones, and then Allison just blurts it out:

"Okay, I'm still nursing three times in the middle of the night and I'm about to lose it." Her eyes are filled with tears, but she is smiling weakly, as if just saying this out loud makes it somehow better.

"Just three times?" Rachel chimes in. "I'd consider that sleeping through the night at this point!"

"Why don't we all check into a hotel and let the guys deal with it for a night or two?" suggests Kate, and we all dissolve into laughter. Not that any of us believe our partners aren't perfectly capable of dealing with a flailing, wailing tot, but the unspoken truth is that we know it's us—the moms—who really couldn't handle it.

Within an hour, we are like old friends. We talk and laugh about diaper rash, cracked nipples and our nonexistent sex lives, and discuss which department stores have the best nursing lounges and which bras are easiest to release with one hand.

"Is anyone else still wearing maternity pants?" Kristen asks between giggles.

One by one, her nine new allies silently lift their tops in solidarity, revealing much more than the answer to Kristen's question. My stomach hurts from laughing so hard and the next day my abs are even a little sore. Between these weekly get-togethers and my nursing workouts, I ought to be back in shape in no time.

12

You Want to Have *What?*

Early parenthood, I have discovered, is a time warp. Maybe because it's really the only time in your life you count in weeks. *She's almost fourteen weeks old. It's been twenty-two weeks since I've slept more than three consecutive hours. In another eleven weeks we can start solid foods!*

"It's been fifteen weeks since we've had sex," Joe announces.

"Fourteen weeks and two days!" I correct him, calculating quickly. "We had sex the night before I was induced and she turns fourteen weeks tomorrow." Petty semantics, I realize, but I'm not in the mood. For anything.

"When did the doctor say it's safe?" he asks.

See, I sort of kept that part about the six-week go-ahead to myself.

"Whenever I feel ready," I answer vaguely.

"I'm ready!" he announces.

No kidding. I need another needy human being groping at my body like I need another rear end to wipe. Maybe I could just bake him a nice pie. You know, show him how much I love him. Aw, hell. Who has time for *that?*

"Soon," I promise.

"It'll be quick," he tries to persuade me. But in all honesty, the thought is about as appealing as a bowl of raw liver soup at the moment. It's not bitter resentment that's keeping my libido at bay; I actually find it a bit of a turn-on watching Joe play daddy. It's not even that I'm ashamed of my flabby stomach or leaking boobs—in a weird way I'm almost proud of them now, and my dear husband has made it abundantly clear that he still finds me desirable. The bottom line is that there is not a single invitation you could extend to me right now that I'd choose over an hour of sleep. I don't want to talk on the phone, visit with friends, answer e-mail, watch a movie, go shopping, read a book or attend the Academy Awards on Jude Law's arm (even if he *did* fancy me more than the babysitter). I'm not depressed, I'm not frigid, I just want to sleep.

Unfortunately, my kid does not. I've whittled down my massive stash of sleep books to the two that aren't a) cruel, b) stupid or c) completely contradictory. The remaining consensus suggests I've got a minimum of two to three months (that's roughly eight to thirteen weeks in new-mom speak) of hell stretching ahead of me before I can expect her to fall—or be pushed—into anything resembling a regular sleep pattern. I don't even have the energy to cry.

"I need a break," I moan to Joe. For the seventh time today, I have managed to rock-dip Sophie into a temporary slumber. The rock-dip is a move I discovered quite by accident—I was pacing back and forth doing the basic rock motion, but I got a cramp in one foot and started to dip—and it miraculously caused her to drift off. So now it's my signature technique. My friend Matt swears the only way his daughter Lily would fall asleep is if he stood with one foot in the bathroom and one in the hall and shifted her from side to side, in and out of the bathroom. Something about the sound of the fan, he suspects. I say if it works once, it's worth repeating.

"Why don't you go upstairs and try to get some rest?" Joe suggests. You see, he's not really a jerk. He just happens to be the only other person in the house who can speak and understand English, so naturally he gets the brunt of the tsunamis that are my mood swings.

"It's not the location," I explain. "I could pass out standing up at a Chili Peppers concert. It's just that the minute I fall asleep she'll wake up, and that's just torture. I think it's better not to fall asleep at all."

"Whatever you say, baby." Joe is a smart man—smart enough to know there's no point in trying to reason with a lunatic.

Sophie is a remarkably happy baby, considering the fact that according to The Books—which claim that any nap lasting less than thirty minutes doesn't "count" as sleep—she's been awake for roughly ninety-eight days straight. She gurgles and coos and lolls about, wearing a perpetual, heartbreakingly dopey grin.

"I want to be you," I tell her when no one else is around. "I want to be rocked and carried and swaddled and tickled and hugged and have my rear end powdered for me." She laughs at this, and then proceeds to spit up down the front of the only clean shirt I own that fits me. I lay her gently in the nearby beanbag and pull the slimy shirt over my head. In the approximately three seconds that transpire during this motion, she is out cold. I stand over her, just watching. Should I try to move her to her crib? Get a damp washcloth and wipe those two drops of spit-up off of her chin? Tuck a blanket around her? Reposition some of the beans so she'll be more comfortable?

Are you a complete moron? a little voice inside my head screams.

Right, sorry, I answer the voice silently. Never content to let well enough alone, I ever so slowly drag the beanbag across the living room until it is adjacent to the sofa. Not a peep passes her angelic lips.

I lie down on the sofa and close one eye. She lets out a soft grunt and the eye flies open. False alarm. I look at the clock. 1:10. Then the phone rings.

Omigod, omigod, omigod.

I have no idea where the phone is. I jump up and dash toward the kitchen, spot it on the hall table and snatch it up on the third ring.

"Hello?" I whisper, tiptoeing back to the living room. Sophie is lying in her beanbag cocoon, eyes closed, unmoving.

"Jenna? It's me. Were you sleeping?" I can hear the smile in Joe's voice.

"Of course not!" I bark. "What time is it?"

"It's five-thirty," Joe replies. "I'm on my way home and wanted to see if my girls needed anything."

"*Five-thirty?*" I shout. "In the *afternoon?*"

I drop to my knees next to Sophie and my heart stops. She's not moving. Joe says something I don't hear because I'm busy staring at her tiny chest. There it is! A soft rise and fall. She's alive. She's just— praise the heavens—asleep.

"You did get some rest," Joe laughs.

"A few minutes maybe," I lie. Why do I feel guilty for taking a nap? Because she could have suffocated in that damned beanbag? Because I was so tired that for all I know she could have been gagging, choking or screaming her head off the entire time and I just never heard it?

I hang up with Joe and quickly call my friend Shelly. Shelly's daughter just turned one, so clearly Shelly knows everything.

"Evalina took naps in a beanbag all the time," she tells me. "It was like a second womb. She'd still sleep in it if I let her."

"But the books say *never* to let a baby sleep on anything soft," I sob. "What if she died?"

"She didn't die," Shelly replies. "Jenna, you're the mom. The book people have to make sweeping, overcautious generalizations, because if they don't, stupid people will flop their babies down into beanbags and then go next door to their neighbors' house for dinner. You were *right there.* She was fine. Sometimes you have to say 'Screw what the books say' and trust your instincts."

My instincts. Right. Still unsure, I confess the whole story to Joe the minute he gets home.

"Good for you guys," he says, giving me a warm hug. "You both needed that, huh?" No reprimand, no what-if lecture like I would have given him, just sweet, unconditional love and support. Not only am I a horrible mother, but now I am a terrible wife, too.

"Want to have sex tonight?" I offer. Well, honestly, it's the least I can do.

"Really?" he asks, as if I just inquired as to whether he might like to have a winning ticket for the state lottery.

"Only if you were serious about the quick part," I tell him.

"You have no idea," he promises.

· ·

trip tip

"Take Me Now, Big Guy!" and Other Things You Won't Be Saying Anytime Soon

THIS IS AN ACTUAL POSTING I read recently on a parenting web site:

"I gave birth a week ago at home. My midwife gave me a clean bill of health and I'm anxious to make love with my husband. Is it really necessary to wait six weeks?"

As if the query itself isn't shocking enough, wait until you hear the response from the "expert":

trip dip

"Your question is very appropriate because many women are anxious to resume an active sex life soon after giving birth."

They are? I find this extremely hard to believe.

Several informal polls (conducted by me) indicate that the question above a) is obviously fake, and b) was written by a horny, hopeful new father.

"Sex? No thanks…but ask me again in a year or two," says my friend Lauren, a two-month veteran of motherhood. "I'd rather chew my own hand off at the wrist," adds my no-nonsense pal Ellen, who is four weeks ahead of Lauren on the path to physical and emotional recovery. Still, your partner's relentless begging and the perpetual pressing of his boner into your backside eventually may wear you down. Before you give in, it may ease your mind a bit to peruse the following answers to some frequently asked questions regarding post-baby sex. (Please note: At the time of this writing, I have one child whom I delivered vaginally. I have no idea about cesarean section births, multiple births, adoption or surrogate deliveries. Also, I live in California, and everyone knows we're weird out here.)

Will it hurt? Let's just say *yes*. Postpartum hormones are not very sex-friendly. The Extreme Science web site lists South America's Atacama Desert as the driest place on earth. I am going to guess that this is only because no Extreme Scientists have ventured between the legs of any new moms lately. Trust me, you'll want to invest in several gallons of lubricant before you even entertain the idea of getting jiggy. They even make flavored lubes that aren't altogether repulsive, which is a great idea for women who aren't quite in the mood yet but might be tempted by a bit of fat-free dessert.

Will it feel different? Oh yeah, but possibly not in the way you think. Although I was right there when it happened, every time I look at my daughter's cantaloupe-size head (never mind her linebacker-like shoulders), I still have trouble believing that she came out of my honey pot. And while I have no intention of inspecting it to be sure, I suspect my honey pot therefore must be the vaginal equivalent of Dr. Banner's poor pants after he has morphed into the Incredible Hulk. *I won't even feel my husband in there,* I think foolishly. *I should have been doing those damned Kegel exercises they told me to do.* Turns out there is absolutely no need for this. The thing is tighter than security at a presidential debate. I am not sure why or how this is the case for me (or whether or not it will be for you), but at least I no longer have distressful images of my own personal Grand Canyon down there. See the bit about lube, above.

What about birth control? What about it? Yes, you need it, even if your period hasn't resumed. (This is assuming, of course, you are not actively shooting for Irish Twins, in which case I urge you to see a mental health professional immediately. Seriously. Something's not right.) In my opinion, condoms or spermicide are the best postpartum methods of birth control. First of all, they contain no unnecessary hormones, something you definitely are not deficient in at the moment. Plus they offer an extra measure of lubrication, which is a nice bonus. Finally, since these two methods are employed in the moment, you are unlikely to forget to use them, a fact that goes a long way toward increasing their odds of successfully preventing another pregnancy.

I am too tired to have sex. Of course you are! For heaven's sake, you haven't had a good night's sleep in probably

trip tip

close to a year. Nevertheless, since your partner's own shuteye has barely been interrupted, he cannot even begin to fathom the depth of the exhaustion you are feeling. In fact, having witnessed your body perform the universe's most incredible feat, he may be feeling even more amorous than usual toward you. That's why it is important to assure him that you still love him and are attracted to him, even though you will go Lorena Bobbitt on his ass if he tries to probe you with his morning monument *one more time.* Explain to him that the best way to maintain your intimacy—without going to the extreme of having actual intercourse—is for him to repeatedly tell you how beautiful you are while simultaneously administering no-strings-attached back and foot rubs. Make it clear that throwing the random load of laundry from the washer into the dryer is a new form of foreplay. In return, grant him permission to order as many adult pay-per-view movies as necessary for the duration. Maybe he'll even pick up a new trick or two. As hard as this is to believe right now, you might appreciate this at some distant point in the future.

What if I'm just not interested in sex? Then your body is doing its job. Think about the magnificent intelligence involved in the design of the female body: You can create and bear another human being! You can sustain that human being with food made in and dispensed directly from your own breasts! Has it occurred to you that there's a *reason* your brilliant bones want a break right now? Babies are demanding! If you are working on top of doing the whole mommy thing, multiply your weariness by infinity. And the thing is, fatigue and friskiness aren't very compatible. Possibly you are still healing from the trauma of delivery. Probably you are feeling a little resentful that your entire life feels as if it got tossed into a blender while your partner's hardly seems affected at all. Yesterday, your only domestic job was to seduce (and wash the occasional dish). Today you have to keep a very small and utterly helpless person alive, happy and dry. It's enough to compel any gal to burn her copy of *The Complete Idiot's Guide to Amazing Sex*. Give yourself a break, okay?

When will my sex drive return? If my experience is in any way indicative, not one minute before—but hopefully within a few months of—the day your baby starts sleeping through the night. The bottom line is if you had a decent sex life before, you will have one again. You won't look as good as you used to in your skimpy lingerie, but then again, your partner's eyesight will probably have deteriorated some by then, which in my mind is absolute proof of divine design.

trip tip

13

We Need a Bigger House to Hold All of This Crap

Babies only need sleep, milk and love. Unfortunately we didn't get the memo. Bottles, booties, bibs, bouncy seats, play mats, pacifiers, plush toys, swings, slings, swaddle wraps, wash cloths and wipe warmers are clogging every available inch of cabinet and closet space in the house. Baskets overflow with diapers and designer receiving blankets and tubs of expensive lotions and potions designed to keep her flawless, milky skin that way for all of eternity. My three-month-old daughter has more shoes than I do, more toys than Toys "R" Us, more blocks than brain cells (and this is no insult to her central nervous system, I can assure you). The child has a cashmere Juicy sweater, for Pete's sake. *A cashmere. Juicy. Sweater.* Okay, I bought it on eBay (new with tags! Score!) for a fraction of the preposterous retail price, but still. *I* don't own a Juicy sweater—in any material.

To understand why all of this is relevant, I'll give you a little backstory: If it is possible for a kid to be bad at playing Barbies, I was. I had about a hundred of the anatomically improbable hotties growing up and I spent countless hours playing stylist. I'd give them all names (Claire and Jessica were always in the mix), brush their silky, synthetic hair and set about choosing the day's duds. Once the lineup was impeccably outfitted—down to the last tiny, perpetually pointed toe—I was done. Between my sister and me, I am pretty certain we had every Barbie accessory ever invented. We had a summer cottage, a winter chalet, a three-story shopping center complete with a work-ing (manual) elevator, a hair salon, a pool, several cars, an airplane, a smattering of furniture, even a ski boat. And still, I couldn't for the life of me figure out what to *do* with the dolls once they were dressed. It never occurred to me to send them on outings, create fictitious life stories, dream up dialogue or use their arsenal of accoutrements as anything other than a backdrop for imaginary photo shoots. (Years later, when I brought the issue up to a group of girlfriends, most admitted they skipped the whole outfitting business altogether and simply forced their stripped-down Barbies, and the occasional Ken, to hump. Over and over and over, they'd mash together pairs of perfect plastic bodies; when this task grew tiresome, they'd stuff the naked dolls back into their toy boxes and whip out Candy Land or Chutes and Ladders. Who knew?)

I am not proud to admit this, but my Mattel mentality apparently has persisted: Once she's adorably dressed, I'm stumped. Maybe I'm just not creative, I think, turning once again to the Internet for inspiration. I Google "activities for babies," but all of the listings either want to sell me something I already have (and have grown bored of), or suggest taking my child to a park, for a walk or to the zoo. *I am not a moron!* I shout to my indifferent computer screen. *I know where to take her! I just don't know what to do with her.* Beyond the basic coochie-coochie-coo, we really don't have much to talk about.

"Want to listen to music?" I ask Sophie, who is lying flat on her back on her inaptly named "activity mat." Nothing. "Look at the cute puppy dog!" I try, wagging a puffy, stuffed Pomeranian in front of her face. A deer in headlights has nothing on this kid. In a fit of despair, I toss the Pomeranian into the air and it lands on my head. Sophie erupts into a cacophony of snorts and giggles. Encouraged, I repeat the move and again, she's delighted. Again and again I pummel my skull with the plush pup, and even thirty bonks later it's as if I've just invented the world's best trick. I am Ray Romano, Chris Rock and Will Ferrell rolled into one! *Is this what other moms do all day long?* I wonder, incredulous. Unbelievable.

"I'm terrible at this," I confess to my sister on the phone. Laurie has a five-year-old and a nine-year-old, and she's always made motherhood look not only easy, but utterly fulfilling.

"It gets easier, Jen," she promises. "Sing songs to her. Roll on the floor with her. Stack blocks and knock them down. It's just about spending time with her. She's learning every minute, just from the sound of your voice. You're bonding all the time, and you're teaching her to feel comfortable and loved."

"But..." I stammer. "All day long?" I mean, honestly. I don't think I can *do* this.

"The days are long, but the years are short," Laurie reminds me. She's always been the annoyingly wise one in the family. "Before long she'll be going off to school, and even when she's home she might not want to hang out with you. Enjoy this time, really. Everyone says it because it's true: It goes by in a blink."

I look at my beautiful, perfect, physically and emotionally undeveloped daughter and genuinely cannot fathom that she is going to become...a person. I ask my sister when, exactly, it will happen.

"One night when you're sleeping," she laughs. There's no answer, of course; it's already happening. In a matter of months Sophie has learned to smile, laugh, find her thumb and her toes, recognize the sound of her name, suckle from a bottle and even roll from front to back. Her first science fair project can't be that far off.

I've never been good at just *being,* but I make a mental commitment to try to live in these moments. To enjoy the run rather than racing for the finish line. Clichés storm my brain: It's the journey, not the destination. If you don't know the way, walk slowly. A journey of a thousand miles begins with a single step.

Any port in a storm, I add despairingly, tossing the Pomeranian into the air for the seven hundredth time today. Once again, hilarity ensues.

Laughter is the best medicine.*

Unless you have pink eye, in which case you should probably see a doctor.

14

....

Parents Say (and Do) the Darnedest Things

The Pomeranian toss turns out to be but the first in an endless string of silly techniques Joe and I begin to employ to earn that magical, musical giggle. We devise methods of soothing, systems for inducing sleep, schemes to stop crying jags, routines for encouraging full, satisfying feedings—each more ridiculous than the last. *Do all parents do these things?* we muse, and *Is this what we went to college for?*

At nap time or when our arms need a break from holding her, we gently place our perfectly swaddled babe in her bassinette—the one that came conveniently equipped with wheels. At first, I imagined the wheels were simply there in the event the parents decided to, for instance, haul their sleeping infant from the bedroom to the living room in order to keep her close by at all times. Turns out, Sophie loves nothing more than when we use these mobility-makers to simulate her own personal Mr. Toad's Wild Ride.

Joe sits on the bed and I sit on the window seat, and with every ounce of force we possess, we hurtle the thing back and forth between us at mach speed, Sophie squealing with delight. If Joe's not home, I plant my feet shoulder-width apart and, gripping the end of the bassinette by her feet, whirl her to and fro, side to side, as one might a particularly dusty throw rug. She can't get enough. Sometimes, centrifugal force (or maybe boredom or nausea, but I guess we'll never know) forces her eyes closed, and more than once she falls asleep during the ride. The bummer in these instances is that the only thing that will *keep* her asleep is continued spinning, and my current lack of fitness usually translates into a disappointingly brief slumber.

We read books to her every day—silly, sing-songy tomes that sometimes spark her interest. We make up countless songs about her, the more nonsensical the better. Our favorite is one we sing to the tune of "Oh My Darling Clementine": *Sophie Bella ain't a fella, she's our little baby girl... She is pretty like a kitty, and she's furry like a squirrel.* She laughs because we laugh, and it feels like we are doing a fine job.

When she's struggling with sleep, we've found that if we use her stuffed bunny's ears to gently stroke down her nose and across her eyebrows, sometimes a nap ensues. Reaching the solid REM sleep state using this method can take upwards of thirty minutes, so one is left wondering if she'd have naturally fallen asleep during that time anyway without the facial massage. Still, we're not taking any chances.

When Sophie does sleep, she likes to sleep to music. Okay, this isn't entirely proven. But *we* like Sophie to sleep to music because this enables us to perform frequent breathing checks without waking her. A friend gives us a CD featuring a track titled "restaurant ambiance" (no lie), which is little more than a continuous loop of dishes and utensils clanging and banging over the raucous conversations of dozens of diners. The point of this, presumably, is to get little ones used to dozing in high-decibel environs so that parents might confidently and peacefully invite them along on outings. It makes sense in theory, but the sound is so grating I finally toss it in the trash. Another CD, a collection of nursery rhymes in both French and English, is almost palatable, so I enter it into the rotation. It never leaves. From tuning in on the baby monitor, Joe and I soon know all of the words by heart.

Alouette, gentille alouette! Alouette, je te plumerai. Je te plumerai la tête. Je te plumerai la tête. Et la tête, et la tête, alouette, alouette, oh, oh, oh, oh…. We croon the words in the car, at our desks, over the dinner dishes, in bed at night. The damned tune is stuck permanently in our heads. I try to forget the literal translation, which I learned through my otherwise useless French Studies minor: *Lark, lovely lark. Lark, I am going to pluck you. I am going to pluck your head, I am going to pluck your head. Pluck your head, pluck your head, lovely lark, lovely lark, oh, oh, oh, oh!* Again and again, we go through the poor bird's entire body—nose, eyes, neck, wings, back, legs—plucking with abandon. Unperturbed by the violent lyrics, Sophie snores peacefully. Friends who pop by with any regularity begin to learn the words and absentmindedly sing along with us.

Although we seem to be making some progress on the snoozing front, during her wake periods Sophie is getting harder to pacify. Maybe she needs a pacifier! My friend Shelly, the expert mom of one, suggests buying several different styles and sizes, as apparently kids can be picky about their suckling toys. (I find this hard to believe as Sophie has no problem slurping on her own toes, but like I said, Shelly knows best.) We've got pointy, glow-in-the-dark models, squishy hospital-issue styles, rigid made-in-Japan designs decked with strange, unrecognizable cartoon characters. None appear to be as appealing as her extreme digits.

Thinking perhaps she needs some help learning to manage this new device, I concoct a brilliant new swaddling technique where the top of the blanket wraps up and around her chin. By doing this, sometimes I can wedge one of the pacifiers between her mouth and the fold to help hold it in place. Immediately, Sophie recognizes a challenge: She spits the pacifier out and the blanket immediately nudges it back into her mouth. She's amused for a minute, and then she starts to get mad.

Two weeks, thirty-seven tantrums (Sophie's) and one near-nervous breakdown (mine) later, I'm at the end of my rope. "You should get a trampoline!" my friend Kim insists.

"She can barely hold her head up," I reply. "I hardly think she's ready for a trampoline."

"No, silly. *You* jump on the trampoline and hold her. That was the only thing that would calm Evan when he was cranky."

I go online and order one of those mini "personal trampolines" for a not-outrageous cost of $39—plus an extra $40 for overnight delivery. (Yeah, I know, I should have kept the birthing ball. *Now* you tell me.) Still, $79 seems a more than reasonable price to pay for my sanity.

When the box arrives the next day, I rip it open right in the living room, Styrofoam peanuts flying everywhere. Sophie, as she's taken to doing, is screaming wildly. She's just eaten, her diaper is dry and it's not quite time to nap, so obviously it's the ever-popular "pissed off for no apparent reason" wail. I screw on the legs in record time, snatch her up and hop on. Instant silence. Could it be this easy?

Easy, it turns out, is a relative term. To say Sophie likes the trampoline is like saying fish are fond of water. She smiles and coos while I hop, bounce, twist and jump until I am breathless and dripping cold sweat. It's worth mentioning that this is the first activity remotely resembling exercise that I have engaged in since early in my pregnancy (not including the marathon of delivery, which unfortunately doesn't really train you for much other than subsequent deliveries), so I'm winded pretty quickly. Beyond that, little droplets of pee seem to be eeking out—of me, not Sophie!—with every few jumps, which makes my workout both exhausting and distressful. Honestly, if you think there's even a remote chance you might find yourself on a trampoline at some point before you die, you might want to consider doing those damned Kegel exercises that everyone talks about but no one actually does.

When I'm too tired to bounce any more, we resort back to the ridiculous stuffed animal games. A perennial favorite is when one of us tucks the tail of her plush pig into the back waistband of our pants and, well, shakes our respective rear end in her face. Honestly, I'd tell you if I could pinpoint where or how this move originated, but seemingly out of nowhere it's just something we do to amuse her.

"I've got to be losing weight," I gasp in Joe's direction one night. He's on the couch, I'm on the trampoline. I'm not being a martyr; Sophie decided early on that she prefers to hop only in my arms, so I'm the Olympic low-jumper in the house. There's no sense trying to relax while Joe bounces with a screeching baby. Tonight I've been hopping for over an hour. Maybe Sophie wants her mom to be in really good shape.

"Have you weighed yourself lately?" he asks.

"No," I confess. "My sweats are falling off, but it could be because I haven't washed them in a few days."

The next day I step on the scale, just for grins. I've lost eight more pounds! That's twenty down...and only twenty-seven to go. Fortunately I don't have time to dwell on this depressing thought. I have a pig-butt dance to do.

trip tip

Mommy's Dead: Fun and Enlightening Tales for Tots

MY FAVORITE "URBAN LEGENDS" WEB SITE insists that the time-honored nursery rhyme "Ring Around the Rosie" is not, as myth suggests, a song about children carrying flowers in their pockets to mask the stench of death that permeated the air during the Black Plague. No, it's just a bunch of silly words strung together, like "a tisket, a tasket" or "hey diddle, diddle." Fair enough. But what about the unfortunate, tumbling "Rock-a-bye Baby"? Or poor, irreparable Humpty Dumpty? And Jack and Jill with their fractured skulls? And that guy who dies in his sleep in "It's Raining, It's Pouring"?

Classic children's literature is hardly better. Am I the only person who had nightmares for four years after hearing the *Hansel and Gretel* tale? The first time my mom read me *Charlotte's Web* I was afraid to leave her side for weeks. Sure, there are crazy folks in the world who try—sometimes successfully—to enslave and eat children. And yes, all living things die. That's life. But can't these joyful little lessons wait until our kids are a teeny bit older?

And while we're on the subject, why are the mothers *always* dead in the princess stories? (Presumably, from a writer's standpoint, this is because killing off the mother opens up a plot slot for the invariably evil stepmother, a dangerous concept to be introducing in this age of blended families, if you ask me.) Name *one* fairy-tale princess who has a kind, loving birth mother in attendance when she marries the handsome prince with whom she will go on to live in infinite bliss, and

I'll send you a check for $10,000.* At least most of the prin-
cesses' mothers are long gone by the time the story even starts,
so our youngsters are spared that small bit of immediate grief.
Animal-lovers get to watch Bambi's mother kick the bucket
practically in the opening scene. Nemo's, too.

It's not just literary death and violence that bug me. Half
the time when I'm skimming through the children's book section at Borders, I have to put something back not because it's
boring or poorly written (although there are plenty of those),
but because of the horrible behavior they seem to condone.
Every other story features a kid talking back, lying, disobeying
authority, skipping school, throwing tantrums or sneaking out
of the house. (Angelina Ballerina clearly doesn't live in New
York City or she'd be a dead sewer rat being cannibalized
by her filthy subway vermin family, which come to think of
it, would make a wonderful children's book!)

Do I really want to read these sorts of things to my
child? Even the classic *Carl the Dog* series relies on a running
plotline of mom leaving baby with the pet Rottweiler while
she jets off to shop/sip cocktails/stroll the streets with her
friends. The *only* words in these books are generally mom's
parting ones: "Look after the baby, Carl. I'll be back shortly."
So it's not like baby and dog conspired to sneak out unsu-
pervised, or mom got locked out of the house/mall/park
and the precocious pair went looking for trouble. *That selfish
tramp is intentionally leaving her baby in the care of a dog!* And
a Rottweiler, no less! (Note to *Carl's* creator: The American
Veterinary Medical Association considers Rottweilers to be
the country's deadliest breed of dog. I'm just saying.) Frankly
I'm surprised Carl's not a cobra.

Good, healthy stuff.

My sister Laurie doesn't ban any of these books or movies. Rather, she uses them as "teaching tools" with her children (ages five and nine) because they present opportunities to point out discipline and parenting styles that "we don't agree with." The death part she addresses matter-of-factly, because she went to medical school and has no problem being cavalier about subjects I can't even contemplate. (Her children: "Where's the mom?" Laurie: "Dead. This is set when? Late eighteenth century? I'm guessing famine.") Fortunately I have a while before Sophie starts asking me any tough questions like "But *why* do the stepmother and stepsisters hate beautiful, kind Cinderella, Mommy?" ("You see sweetie, women can be incredibly petty, and you might as well face the fact now that pretty gals are frequently the victims of jealous wrath.")

In the meantime, I'm dusting off my now-antique Dr. Seuss collection. Trust me, *There's a Wocket in my Pocket* only *sounds* dirty. And sure, the Grinch may steal Christmas—but everyone knows Whoville isn't a real place, and besides, they get it back. Although, come to think about it, Sally and Whatshisname were awfully young to be left alone in the house on that cold, cold, wet day when the Cat in the Hat showed up and turned the place upside down.

Forget it. I'm writing my own children's books. They'll feature obedient children from functional, two-parent households where nobody dies or locks anyone in a dungeon, even as a joke. Please check www.jennamccarthy.com soon for available titles.

* *Offer not valid anywhere in the U.S. or, now that I think about it, the world. I was just making a point, but honestly I cannot think of a single one. So shoot me if I'm wrong. I'm exhausted, okay?*

15

....

Sleep in Heavenly Peace
(Please!)

We celebrate Sophie's four-month birthday not with a cake (she's not eating solid foods yet, and I certainly don't need the calories), but with a plan: Tonight, we are going to allow her to soothe herself into a long and peaceful sleep.

This sounds gentler—and easier—than it turns out to be.

But prevailing wisdom (and by this I mean the opinion I'm choosing to subscribe to) suggests it is appropriate to allow a baby of this age to learn the very important skill of falling asleep. Who knew this was a skill? I thought it was pure biology—you get tired, your eyelids get heavy, you let them close and you wake up eight or twelve hours later. *Sounds* simple, but no. Apparently little tykes get rabidly addicted to the rocking, singing, bouncing, swaddling, nursing, cuddling and sometimes driving around the block we do to help them drift off to la-la land. Taking away these crutches can result in withdrawal symptoms you'd expect from a dispossessed crack addict: shuddering, wailing, vomiting, clawing and generalized, inconsolable hysteria.

But since the alternative is to continue to rock/sing/bounce/ swaddle/nurse/cuddle/drive her for all of eternity, a few days (or weeks) of unmitigated, hair-pulling madness seems a small price to pay. So here we are, gearing up to let her "cry it out."

I am already anticipating and preparing for the onslaught of angry letters I am going to receive for including this account and, more importantly, for choosing this method of sleep training in the first place. Please let me remind you, as I tell myself every day now, that there are a million different ways to parent. What works for one parent or one child doesn't necessarily work for the next. And quite frankly, even if you've been there, it's important not to judge other people because I'm pretty sure self-righteousness is a sin (if it isn't, it ought to be because it's extremely annoying). And if you *haven't* been there, allow me to suggest that you never, ever, say "never," unless you are particularly fond of eating crow, which—and trust me because I know—tastes *nothing* like chicken.

On the appointed night, I nurse Sophie as always, read her my favorite bedtime story, *The Going to Bed Book,* for good measure, put a fresh diaper and a thick smear of diaper cream on her, and swaddle her within an inch of her life. She looks up at me and gurgles. Poor thing has no idea what's coming. I feel like a callous shepherd leading a clueless little lamb to the slaughter.

"You ready?" I ask Joe as I head for the nursery with the human cocoon-with-a-head that is our daughter.

"I guess," he replies nervously. I've explained how this is going to go down: Of the two basic "cry it out" plans to choose from, I have decided to begin with the more hard-core one, called—I learn with no small amount of alarm—"extinction." This means, quite simply, you put the child in her crib, leave the room and don't return, under *any* circumstances, until the appointed wake-up time. At this age, that's eight hours from now. I can listen to screaming for eight hours, I figure, bracing myself for the worst-case scenario.

Looks like I figured correctly.

The minute I close her door, the wails begin. And really, why shouldn't they? I look at it from her perspective: This isn't how things usually transpire. And human instinct is to protest when something out of the ordinary happens. Have you ever been left standing on the shore of a deserted island while the only boat in the world—the one your friends, family and dog are on—pulls away? Well, if you had, I doubt you would have just stood there and shrugged. No, you probably would scream. And shout. And flail your arms. Maybe even jump up and down. If you happened to have a flare in your pocket, I'm sure you would fire it up at a breathtaking pace. "Hey guys!!!" you'd bellow until the tug disappeared over the horizon and your throat bled from the effort. "You forgot me!!!"

It breaks my heart to think that Sophie might think I have forgotten her.

"I have to go in there," I tell Joe, looking at my watch. The books suggest keeping strict tabs on the time, and now I see why: It has been exactly three minutes. If you had held a gun to my head, I would have sworn that at least three hours had elapsed. Maybe more. Three lousy minutes? I lie down on the couch and wrap the fattest cushion around my head. Sophie's wails cut through those six inches of down filling like a hot knife piercing a stick of butter.

"I can't do this, I can't do this, I can't do this," I moan, mostly because it's true, but also because the sound slightly muffles Sophie's sobs, which are definitely getting louder and more frantic.

"What's the alternative?" Joe asks.

"*Modified* extinction," I answer, jumping up with renewed hope. "Actually, I was thinking this way sounded much better anyway."

Modified extinction is a watered-down version of crying-it-out that allows the parent or parents to check in on the child at regular intervals. The key is to gradually increase the time between soothing stints. This way, the theory goes, the baby knows that you haven't forgotten her, so she doesn't have to feel abandoned (and you don't have to worry her little arm is stuck through the crib slats or her skin is caught in the zipper of her pajamas or her blanket is wrapped around her neck). This seems much more humane—for everyone involved. So after watching the clock for ten solid torturous minutes, I pop in for a visit.

The instant Sophie sees me, her shrieks escalate.

"Shhhh, shhh, shhhh, baby. I'm here," I tell her, standing by her crib. Of course, she's broken Houdini-style out of her cocoon, despite the fact that I have become somewhat of a swaddling savant. I *shhh* and *shhh,* and she wails and flails and looks at me with hungry, accusing eyes: *Why are you just standing there?* she demands. The book strictly forbids picking the baby up, even when following the modified-torture method, but I can't resist. I scoop her up and hold her until her sobs become little yelps peppered with hiccups, explaining to her all the while that in a minute I'm going to place her down again so that she can get some sleep, but that I'll be right outside of her door the entire time. I tell her that this is for her own good and that someday she'll thank me, swearing on an invisible stack of Bibles that I won't say the same thing about piano lessons in five years.

I re-swaddle her and hug her to my body, preparing myself for the onslaught. The minute I begin bending over the railing of her crib, she's back to full-blown rage. I set her down as quickly and gently as I can and bolt from the room, crying already. I'm not allowed to go back in for fifteen minutes.

Forty-five seconds. A minute and a half. *I'm not going to look for at least seven minutes,* I vow. I recite the lyrics to "Me and Bobby McGee" in my head to pass the time, then go through the entire "Reading from the Letter of Paul to the Corinthians" speech I gave in church in third grade and cannot for the life of me seem to forget. Confident that at least seven minutes have passed, I glance back at the clock. Four minutes and ten seconds. Eleven unforgiving minutes to go. I bang the heel of my hand on my forehead—hard—and for a minute the smarting stabs of pain block out Sophie's cries.

"Want to watch some TV?" Joe asks.

"No," I tell him, shaking my head sadly. "If she's going to suffer, then I am, too." It's times like this I wish I bit my nails. Or at least knew how to knit.

As the intervals gradually get longer, we learn something interesting about Sophie: The kid is tenacious. We do intervals of twenty, twenty-five, thirty, thirty-five, forty minutes—and she's still going strong. We swaddle, soothe and sneak out over and over. It's almost midnight, and Joe and I are worked. I start to worry that now she's probably starving and will *never* fall asleep.

"Should we just forget this tonight and try again tomorrow?" Joe asks tentatively, echoing the very thought that's bounding around in my brain.

"Maybe..." I say. It's just so hard to know if we've made any progress. Nevertheless, I can't take it anymore tonight. I know that if I retrieve her and bring her into bed with us, she'll nurse herself to sleep within ten minutes. *Ten minutes from now we could all be asleep!* I shuffle to her room feeling like a complete failure.

At the door I notice something strange: It's quiet in there. No sobbing. No whimpering. Not even the occasional hiccup. *She's dead!* The gruesome thought just pops into my head, but honestly, it seems like the only possible explanation for the sudden silence on the other side of the door.

Grateful that we've abandoned the full-extinction madness, I slowly pry the door open and tiptoe in. She looks so peaceful I almost think I was right to worry. But then I see it: the gentle, rhythmic rise and fall of her tiny rib cage. I have to stare at it for a full minute before I am convinced it's not just my eyes playing tricks. I look at her sweet, perfect face, and unbelievably, there's the faintest curve of a smile on her lips.

The fact that we have to do this all over again tomorrow and the next day and the day after that is irrelevant. I fall into my bed, a similar grin gracing my exhausted face, and for four and a half solid, heavenly hours, we sleep.

I hear the birds chirping softly before I am even semi-awake. Actually, they're not chirping, they're cooing. And gurgling. I'm about to ask Joe if he's noticed any new nests in the yard when I realize the bird sounds are coming from Sophie's room. I sprint in there and you could knock me over with a sneeze. She's not yelping or screaming—she's just lying there, looking up at her crib mobile and having a profound conversation with the fluffy little fellows dangling from it. When she senses my presence, she breaks into the biggest grin I've ever seen and her arms and legs spring into their automatic happy octopus dance. She doesn't hate me! She's rested and happy, and she knows how much I love her and she loves me just as much.

It's official: I am the best mother on the planet.

16

···

Why My Pediatrician Has a Summer House and I Don't

I'm proud of the fact that Sophie is five months old and has yet to see the inside of an ambulance or the ER. Since she was birthed by a card-carrying neurotic, this is no minor feat.

And yet I know somewhere in the dark recesses of my brain that even under the most watchful of eyes, eventually *every* baby will suffer a bump, bruise, abrasion or raging 99-degree fever. The phrase "maternal instinct" implies that I should know which of these traumas warrants swift medical attention. I admit I am not altogether confident on this front. But we've been lucky—until now.

The ordeal starts when I lay Sophie down on her changing table one afternoon. I slip her dirty diaper off and am rummaging in the drawer for a clean one when, out of nowhere, she starts making a horrible wheezing, air-sucking sound. *She's choking!* Almost without thinking I leap into action, miraculously remembering the protocol from our now-distant infant CPR class.

Hastily I snatch Sophie up, flip her over onto my forearm so that her face is in my hand and her feet are somewhere around my elbow, tilt my arm down so that her head is lower than her chest and administer several good, solid *thwacks* between her shoulder blades with the heel of my other hand.

A split second of silence is followed by blood-curdling howls, but for once these do not upset me. In fact, the sound is sweeter than a choir of angels belting out Whitney Houston's "I Will Always Love You." If she's screaming, she's not choking! I did it! I kept my cool and managed to dislodge whatever it was that was wedged in her windpipe. I saved her life.

We slump to the floor. Feeling more than a little shaky, I stay there for a bit and hold her and rock her and try to calm the two of us down. When I am reasonably confident that she is breathing normally and that my legs will indeed support my weight when I try to use them, I push myself back up and timidly return her to the changing table.

Straight away she's gripped in another fit of gagging and wheezing. For the love of Pete! It's still *in there!* I can see it in my mind: a shiny new penny that, not coincidentally, happens to be the precise circumference as her windpipe. But it's not lodged in there directly; it's somehow able to pivot—maybe her windpipe is more oval than round?—so that it only chokes her when she's lying down. What could be more obvious?

I repeat the infant-Heimlich procedure and precisely the same events unfold, with the exception of the fact that this time Sophie— whom I have not yet managed to diaper—pees all over me, herself, the changing table and the floor.

Now she's wet, mad, scared and more than a bit disgruntled, and I'm a complete basket case. I call her pediatrician's office and inform the receptionist that I think my baby has something stuck in her throat, possibly a penny. I ask very calmly (not altogether true) if we can be seen immediately. Either the office is particularly slow or I sound particularly convincing (or hysterical) because they tell me they have an opening in a half hour. We are there in seventeen minutes.

After a maddeningly terse examination, Dr. Blasé pronounces Sophie "fine."

"Then why was she gagging?" I demand. *He didn't even look down her throat! Oh, but good thing he looked in her ears. Lots of babies choke on earwax. Why isn't he ordering X-rays? I want X-rays. Lots and lots of them.*

"Sounds like she just discovered a fun new sound to make," Dr. Blasé explains.

"Really?" I say sarcastically, scanning the room for any framed diplomas. Where'd this guy go to med school, Ignoramus U? "Then why does she only do it when I lay her down?" Ha! Riddle me that one, Dr. Dimwit.

"My guess would be that she associates the sound with her changing table or with the experience of having her diaper changed," he replies calmly. "She got a reaction out of you and she remembered it."

"Oh, yeah!" I snicker. "That was fun for her! I'm sure she couldn't *wait* to be smacked around like a punching bag again by her own mother!" Now he's done it. I'm crying. If we're going to have even one more kid, I should really buy stock in Kleenex.

Dr. Blasé smiles wanly. "Jenna, babies aren't very sophisticated. She might not have *enjoyed* your reaction, but she's learning about cause and effect. It's natural for her to test her environment. It's her job."

Although it kills me to admit it, his psychobabble doc-talk sort of makes sense. But just because something is plausible, does that mean it's necessarily true or right? Because I can *see* that penny stuck in her throat! I tell Dr. Blasé this. *If Sophie was HIS kid, I'm sure she'd already be rubbing elbows with the radiologist.*

"Did you see her with a penny?" he asks, changing tacks and barely concealing his disdain.

"Well, no, but—"

"Does she have access to spare change at your house?" he suggests.

"Of course she does!" I bark. Well, for crying out loud. It's not like we live in squalor or anything, but pennies are small! They fall out of pockets and roll under couches and into the nooks between the end tables and the wall, and if I am going to be expected to keep track of every coin on the face of the Earth for the next several decades, I'm going to need a stable of full-time personal assistants and a prescription for Xanax.

"Let's try to stay calm, okay?" Dr. Blasé urges. "Did you see her with anything small in her hand? Or did you see her actually swallow *anything?*"

"No!" I bellow. I am sobbing now. "But it's in there. I just know it."

"Fine, I'll order the X-rays," he mutters, writing something—probably "mom's a whack job"—on Sophie's folder as he leaves. I couldn't care less. I'm not about to put my pride before my child's safety.

I hope that you are sitting down as you read this book, because the shock of this next part could easily knock a person right off her feet: The X-rays turn up…nothing. No penny. No marble, paper clip, petrified grape, crusty cheese cube, rusty thumbtack or jagged-edged beer bottle cap, either. I feel sick and humiliated, and more than anything, confused about what to do now that a coin-ectomy is not on the schedule.

"Well, what am I supposed to do if she does it again?" I demand.

"Talk to her," Dr. Blasé urges.

"Talk to her," I repeat dumbly. "And say what, precisely?"

"Tell her that you don't like it when she makes that sound because it scares you," he says simply. "And then ask her to stop."

Well, that is just flat-out ridiculous, I think, hating myself and Dr. Blasé and this office and all doctors everywhere for being so impossibly smug and dispassionate. *She's five months old! "Please stop?"*

Why don't I just say, "Please tell me why you were gagging? And while you're at it, would you mind changing your own stinky diapers from now on?"

I get the chance to test-drive Dr. Blasé's preposterous plan that very evening. After her bath, I dry her off and we return to the scene of the crime. As soon as she is horizontal, as in a recurring nightmare or dreadful Bill Murray movie, the retching resumes. Instead of immediately flipping her over, I gently pull her into a sitting position.

"Sophie," I say calmly but sternly, lowering my face so that our noses are nearly touching, "I do not like it when you make that sound. It scares me and I'd like you to please stop." I feel like a moron having this conversation with a baby, but I don't know what else to do. She gurgles back at me, and feeling like perhaps we have reached some vague sort of an understanding, I lower her back down. She doesn't gasp, pant or heave. She breathes perfectly normally, the whole episode apparently forgotten. Even more miraculously, she never makes the horrible gagging sound again.

Maybe the timing was pure coincidence. Maybe the talking thing worked after all. Or maybe Sophie managed to swallow the penny before any silly X-ray could find it, a theory I still hold plausible, and if I had the energy and a slightly stronger stomach, I'd scrutinize her poop to prove it.

trip tip

Is my Baby Okay?
(A Field Guide to Overreacting)

AS A NEW PARENT, it is enormously difficult to determine when, if ever, it is appropriate to worry about your infant's seemingly abnormal behavior. After all, it takes a while to establish what's "normal" for him or her, and you may not have had that luxury the first time you feel that twinge of concern. Or you may feel twinges of concern every waking minute of every living day, and despite the fact that you know good and well how that innocent flock of sheep perished because the silly shepherd boy cried wolf one too many times, you just can't seem to relax.

If that's the case, skip over this section because it probably won't help you one bit. It's not your fault if you're a worrywart; you were likely born that way. Or your parents made you into one. The cause of your chronic anxiety is neither here nor there. "It is what it is," as my friend Pam always says, which in this case is just another way of saying "You can't sue your parents for your crappy DNA without looking like a complete jerk, and besides, you'll lose, so why bother?"

Me, I'm a fretter. I fret about every little thing. Motherhood has not had a pleasant or positive impact on this predisposition. I worry when I think Sophie is nursing too long (my milk supply is dwindling!) and when she's not nursing long enough (my milk supply is dwindling!). When she's swaddled, I agonize that she'll overheat; when she's not, I'm afraid she'll freeze. I am concerned she'll get a sunburn when we go outside, but I'm terrified to slather her virgin skin with dangerous chemicals. I'm worried that she'll get teeth soon—can these boobs handle any more abuse?—and at the same time I'm afraid that she won't. Four poopy diapers in a row have me questioning her digestive health, while twenty-four hours without even one sends me on a mad hunt for cures for "infant constipation." (And incidentally, what color is her poop supposed to be? I realize this would be considered a taboo subject if I were talking about my own doo-doo, but seriously. She consumes one thing and one thing only. Shouldn't the subsequent waste matter be one consistent, uniform color? You'd think so, but no. On any given day it might be green, yellow, brown, black, orange, even white. It might be Hope diamond-hard on Tuesday and watery wet on Wednesday, or anything in between. I never manage to get a straight answer as to why this is so, only that—you guessed it—it's all "normal.")

I have polled all of my mom-friends to see how they determine when medical intervention is necessary where their child is concerned. Here's a summary of their hard-won wisdom, including specific things you can do in the event of an emergency:

1. Don't be scared of a little old fever. Fever is a sign that the body is fighting off an infection. To that end, administering Tylenol can actually make her sicker by thwarting this innate self-healing process. Relax and let her body take care of business.

2. Unless, of course, the fever is over 99 degrees—then you can leap into action. Generally speaking, a temperature of less than 102 degrees Fahrenheit isn't considered a major deal, but an elevated temperature could be an early warning

trip tip

sign of any number of conditions that are best treated when caught in a timely fashion. Call your doctor and at least have a phone consultation. You'll feel better.

3. If she gets a little scratch or bug bite, call your doctor. While you are on hold for two hours, you may clean the area gently. Do not use hydrogen peroxide on her skin. I can't remember why, but I know it's bad. Instead, apply a little antiseptic cleanser and then a dab of antibacterial cream to the area. Do not cover it with a bandage, because some babies have latex allergies, and besides, pulling a gummy glue strip off her delicate skin is almost always worse than the original injury. When the doctor finally takes your call, confirm that this was the best course of action.

4. Judge by her demeanor, not her symptoms. If she has diarrhea, flushed cheeks and a lacy rash all over her body, for instance, but is eating and urinating as usual and appears happy, there may be nothing to worry about. But if it makes you feel better, call your doctor anyway, just to be sure. This is why you have health insurance.

5. If she has diarrhea, flushed cheeks and a lacy rash all over her body, who cares how she's acting? That's scary stuff. Call your doctor.

6. If she has diarrhea, flushed cheeks and a lacy rash all over her body, and she's crabby or lethargic, or isn't eating and urinating as normal, get to Urgent Care or the ER immediately. I don't want to alarm you, but this is no time to take her shoe shopping.

7. If she isn't eating and urinating as normal, call your doctor.

8. If no symptoms are present whatsoever, call your doctor. Some illnesses, after all, are completely asymptomatic. Unless you're psychic, how are you supposed to know if she is really fine?

9. Call your doctor just to say hi. She'll appreciate this personal touch and may be more likely to squeeze you in when you call with an emergency tomorrow.

10. Get to know all of the staff at the pediatrician's office by name. This will be easy as you will be there frequently. An occasional basket of muffins or bagels is a nice touch that will ensure you're not remembered as the "neurotic lady who's here every other day," but as "the neurotic lady who's here every other day and brings us food."

11. Get all of her immunizations when the doctor suggests it is appropriate to do so. It's her job to know this stuff, and it's your job to worry about it. You're doing your job brilliantly; now let her do hers.

12. Go to medical school and become a doctor. In the long run, this is probably the cheapest and easiest method of guaranteeing your child receives a lifetime of prompt, high-quality care.

trip tip

17

I've Been to Hell— and It Looks Suspiciously Like My Kitchen

Five months old is a great age for babies. Sophie now can sit and hold her head up—often at the same time. She can drag her body, crippled dog-style, across the carpet and can even activate the sounds and lights on her bouncy seat with her feet. When she's not engaged in such important infant work, she smiles, laughs, claps her hands and rolls over *both ways*. It's like having another person in the house!

Apparently, the other person is getting hungry.

I know this because she is constantly making chewing motions when she sees food—even when there's nothing in her mouth—and trying to snatch scraps off of my plate when she's sitting in my lap. I don't let her actually *eat* anything she grabs, of course, because I am painstakingly familiar with the baby-feeding rules and I know that the approved order of introduction does not start with shake-and-bake chicken or Punjab eggplant.

Beyond her obvious desire for human food, Sophie has mastered the all-important "pincer grasp" motion with her thumb and index finger, which some experts insist is another sign of eating readiness.

I wonder, though, whether her ability to pick up marbles, paper clips and pen caps suggests an eagerness to eat "people food" or just an ability to scare me witless. But it's a sign (because "they" say it is), and that means we can move on to the next stage. I am overjoyed about this fact for one reason above all others: Blessed Mary ever Virgin, the fun bags are about to get a break. I fantasize about the day when I will eventually wear sexy, lacy bras again, the kind that *don't* have leakproof liners.

But long before that day, I'm going to have to teach this kid how to eat. The books and web sites I trust suggest starting with one teaspoon of food per serving. A whole teaspoon? Okay, I know she's small and everything, but I'll bet even lizards eat more than a teaspoon of spider guts at a sitting. This is going to be a piece of, well, pureed squash.

I put Sophie into her new highchair, which suddenly looks cavernous. She lists to one side and I prop her back up. She lists to the other side, so I grab a pair of towels and roll them up, spa-style, under each elbow. Success! She bangs her arms on the tray, the universal "What's for supper?" sign. I slip a bib under her chin and fasten the Velcro in the back. She promptly pulls it off. I reattach it. She rips it off again. Damn that pincer grasp.

Hey, this is a fun game, Mom! Sophie says, silently.

"Talk to baby in an encouraging manner as you feed her," one book suggests. "Keep it light and fun!" recommends another.

"Let's put this bib on so we can keep your pretty top nice and clean," I suggest, sneaking my hands around the back of her neck.

Rip.

"Look at the cute little ducky on your bib! He wants to see what a good eater you are!"

Riiiiiiiiiiiiiiip.

Looks like I need a new approach.

I toss the bib on the counter and pull her shirt over her head. "Who wants to eat naked today?" Why not? It's not like we're trying to impress anyone here with our good manners or fancy dinner attire.

I'm not sure if all babies are so blessed, but it turns out Sophie has an uncanny ability to spit out twice whatever volume of food I manage to get into her mouth. It's not as if she's regurgitating it; the food barely makes its way past her lips before it's out again in duplicate quantities. Here's pretty much how it goes: She opens her mouth like a little bird, and using a miniature rubber-tipped spoon, I gently deposit 1/10 of a teaspoon of watery rice cereal into the hole. One nanosecond later, 1/5 of a teaspoon of liquid dusted with rice cereal comes out of the hole. I quickly scoop the drippings off of her chin and redeposit the new mixture back into her mouth. Out pops close to a half teaspoon of now-foamy froth freckled with an even smaller smattering of cereal particles. We repeat the process for close to an hour until I am convinced that the fare I'm forcing on her is nothing but her own reconstituted saliva, and I abandon the endeavor until the next scheduled "feeding."

Twice a day for the next week we play the spittle game. Occasionally she locks her lips mid-feeding for no apparent reason, and even though I know better, I find myself trying to pry her lips open with the spoon's rubber tip. When I do, she plugs the opening with her tongue, sometimes giving me a raspberry for good measure. She thinks this is hilarious, despite my obvious lack of amusement. I try "Here comes the choo-choo train!" but she clamps her trap shut extra tightly when I do this, possibly because she has no idea what a choo-choo train is or what the tunnel's purpose is in relation to it, or perhaps because I was a famously stubborn kid and what goes around comes around.

Even though I'm lightning fast with the food/drool retrieval, after every feast her face, neck and even armpits look as if they have been spackled with cereal. I quickly learn that if I don't wipe her down before the droppings dry and harden, it takes turpentine and a chisel to clean out those cracks.

(Note to Child Protective Services and people who take things very literally: It doesn't *really* take turpentine and a chisel to clean a food-spattered baby. I mean, that would probably work, but what I'm saying is I never try this. I swear.)

You know what happens when you sit in the same spot in your house for mind-numbing hours at a stretch? You start to notice things. For instance, there are twenty-two vertical slats on the east side of my kitchen wall, but only twenty on the west side! Isn't that crazy? And my ceiling has all sorts of funny spots in it that look like nail holes that were plugged but not sanded before the lazy contractor just painted right over them. Looking at this every day inspires a bored kind of rage in me, but what am I going to do about it? Whip out the sander and some touch-up paint? Hire a handyman? Add it to the endless list of things I'm constantly nagging Joe about? Instead, I count the holes. (There are fourteen.) I marvel at how grossly dusty that little vented panel along the bottom of the refrigerator is, and even more amazingly, how I never noticed any of these things before. As maddening as these pastimes are, anything is better than watching the lethargic clock.

I spoon, Sophie spits. I count slats and holes and dust bunnies and spoon some more. The goop in her bowl gets foamier and runnier. I practice multiplication tables in my head because I once read that brain cells are one of the body's "use 'em or lose 'em" constituents, and the old cerebellum is yet another of my currently under-exercised parts. I conjugate French verbs, paying extra attention to the irregular ones. *Je veux, tu veux, il veut, nous voulons, vous voulez, ils veulent.* I envision my ass spreading to roughly the size of Kansas from the endless sitting, so I try to find some activities I can do on my feet while Sophie finger-paints her tray with cereal. I squeeze my glutes as I scrub my cabinet doors and alphabetize all of the jars and cans in my pantry. Eventually I resort to cleaning the refrigerator vent with an old toothbrush, all the while knowing that I am the only person who will ever notice or appreciate this.

Occasionally I ask Sophie patiently, kindly, if she could pretty please open her sweet little lips so Mommy can give her some yummy food, but nothing doing. I pretend to eat the slop myself, but she couldn't care less. Finally I drop the spoon on her tray in frustration, muttering something along the lines of "I suppose when you get hungry enough, you'll eat."

Really mature, I know.

I march to the sink to begin the inexhaustible cleanup process. Wondering why Sophie isn't clamoring for me or my undivided attention, I turn back to see that she has picked up the spoon and is inspecting it from every angle. I watch in amazement as she drags it expertly through her cereal and maneuvers it up toward her mouth. At the last minute she upends the spoon, but the cereal is sticky, so the bulk of it lands on her tongue despite this rookie move. She laps it up like a kitten, and to my great shock and awe, *none of it comes back out*. Not a morsel. Just like that, she figures out how to eat—and she does it entirely on her own.

It still takes upwards of an hour for Sophie to get a full feeding in this way, and afterwards she looks as if she was egg-dipped and batter-rolled. But I can tell she enjoys the satisfaction of feeding herself, and I can't say I have any remorse about handing over the reins.

Pretty soon we master all of the pureed provisions and move on to finger foods. My daughter is a gourmand! Cheerios, cheese cubes, mini-macaronis, hard-boiled eggs, steamed broccoli florets, plums, pears and peaches go down like marbles on a slide. My diaper bag becomes a chuck wagon with straps, but getting out is so much easier now (knowing that a few Goldfish crackers can thwart a checkout line meltdown) that I don't mind the inconvenience.

Until I discover the downside of constantly carting perishables with you. Sophie and I are trying to get out of the house to run some errands, but I can't find the diaper bag anywhere. I think back to the last time I had it—at the park, when? Yesterday? Day before?—and realize I must have left it in the car. I dash outside, whip open the car door and am almost knocked down by the horrific stench.

Here's the thing: Every new mom will forget, at least once, that there's a Ziploc bag of steamed veggies or poached chicken pieces in her diaper bag. This will invariably happen on the day she leaves the bag in the car in 104-degree heat. For three days. When this happens, please heed my suggestion and *do not* open the bag in an effort to determine precisely what the blue furry stuff inside might once have been. (They were carrots. Does that really matter now?) And don't even try to get the sulfur smell out of the diaper bag, either. It's a lost cause.

The good news is that sometimes even stinky, noxious clouds have silver linings: Even Joe agrees that the bag is history, so I get the green light to buy a new one.

When this happens to you, tell your husband this story. If he still protests the new purchase, stuff the old bag under his nose and threaten to bury it beneath the driver's seat of his car one random night while he's sleeping. He'll come around.

trip tip

Chew on This: A Helpful, Handy Baby-Feeding Primer

IT'S PRETTY MUCH AGREED that as far as food is concerned, babies can get by on breast milk for the first year of life. To me, that's like saying "women can get by with one purse in perpetuity," which—theoretically, of course—is true, but do I really want to carry a sequined silver evening bag roughly the size of a banana on a day trip to Disneyland? Am I expected to tote my lip gloss and compact to the opera (never mind that I don't go to the opera) in my hot pink, laminated, moisture- and mold-resistant, you-could-fit-a-case-of-diet-Coke-in-it diaper bag? And which of these two options—if I am going to be allowed but one—do I bring to a job interview? On a hiking trip? To a funeral?

Armed with a combination of this obviously sound reasoning and the permission of your pediatrician, you will set about researching the best time and means of introducing solid foods (which, frankly, aren't very solid when you start out, but that's another matter altogether). After considerable Googling, you may stumble across this line on a parenting-advice web site: "Mothers often report that they knew their babies were ready when they picked up food from a plate, chewed it, swallowed it and wanted more." As readiness indicators go, I would agree the only thing that could beat that would be if baby tied on her own bib and held up a handwritten recipe for pureed coq au vin.

When you were pregnant, perhaps you made a point of telling people that you planned to make your own baby food.

Why wouldn't you? You know how to boil water and you are fairly certain that your $200 stainless steel wedding-gift blender can handle more than some frozen fruit and a carton of organic yogurt. After exhaustive research, you will discover that you need a master's degree in nutrition just to feed a baby. If you're going to *make* your own baby food, make it a PhD. The safe handling/preparing/storing requirements may be daunting enough to force you to give up, but look on the bright side: Few things say "I love my kid" like forking over for ridiculously overpriced organic baby food you have to drive thirty round-trip miles to purchase.

Still, even when your pantry is stocked Andy Warhol-style with a rainbow of tiny jars of all-natural edibles, you can't just open and dispense these rations willy-nilly. Oh no, there are rules: First and foremost, one must always start with single-grain cereals (rice, barley or oat, but not wheat before her first birthday because it can trigger allergies). These cereals must be iron fortified and can be mixed alone (but never together) with water, formula or breast milk. I genuinely and enthusiastically applaud the women who opt for breast milk as their mixer of choice. For me, one of the greatest advantages of feeding Sophie "real" food is that my tired, saggy boobs are going to get a much-needed break. I will continue to nurse her the other four or eight times a day her little tummy demands it, but when we're in the kitchen, the milk jugs will be out to lunch.

Once you've determined how you will liquefy your cereal choice, you must introduce it solo for several days, making sure to look for signs of allergic reactions—the most common of which are rash and diarrhea. Since babies frequently develop rashes and diarrhea anyway, it may take you several months or years to be sure that your baby is indeed tolerant of a particular grain.

Once you have made your way through the grain choices, you are encouraged to move on to cooked, mashed vegetables (but yellow before green—I am not sure why, especially since G comes before Y in the alphabet, so this is very hard to remember—and not carrots because they contain relatively high levels of nitrates, and even though nitrate poisoning is extremely rare, the nickname "blue baby syndrome" is enough to scare a person off of them forever). After baby has been successfully—and without asthmatic incident—introduced to a colorful assortment of vegetables, you can progress to fruits (but not strawberries or oranges because they, too, are highly allergenic, and not grapes because the skins make them little round death traps, even if you dice them into pieces so small you can actually see the little protons and electrons bouncing around in the pulverized nuclei). Last in the baby food lineup are meats (always well cooked and strained, but never, ever hot dogs, which are essentially the carrots of the protein world, being that they pack an unhealthy dose of those potentially poisonous nitrates). And for heaven's sake, do not give baby *even one bite* of your processed cheese doodads or maple nut scone because they might contain honey or corn syrup, both of which contain "bacterial spores that cause food-borne illnesses," which can be (dear God) fatal in infants.

Are you getting all of this? Taking notes? Wait! It's not over yet. You must never feed a baby directly from the baby food jar, as doing so can introduce bacteria from the baby's mouth into her food, where it will reproduce and proliferate like drunken rabbits on spring break. This is presuming she won't eat the entire contents of the jar, which, of course, she

trip tip

trip tip

will if—and only if—you transfer it into a bowl. As with breast milk or formula, parents are cautioned never to heat baby food in the microwave because of those hazardous "hot spots" nuked food can develop. I say don't heat her food at all, by any means, ever. This isn't something I do to be cruel; it's a handy trick my friend Barbara taught me. When your baby eats food for the first time, she has no idea what to expect. But if you give it to her heated up from the get-go, you're unintentionally creating a warmed-food snob. More importantly, you're up the creek if you're forced to serve it up cold, say, in a restaurant or during a blackout.

It is important to stop feeding your baby when she is full. "A baby who is full will close or cover its mouth with its hands, turn its head away, shake its head 'no' or cry," explains yet another grammatically challenged web site. (A baby is not an "it"!) Again, since babies often perform these exact actions when they are hungry, tired, frustrated, sick or just trying to play a nice game of peek-a-boo, you may have to rely on your instincts here.

Other than seeing that she's getting enough but not too much, watching her sugar and salt intake, closely monitoring all of the expiration dates on her assortment of edibles and making sure your "helpful" mother-in-law doesn't sneak her a peanut or slice of bacon when you're not looking, that's about it. You should be well on your way to a wonderful feeding experience!

18

....

Time Isn't the Only
Thing That's Crawling

Since Sophie is for the most part stationary, I've found that I can sit her on a blanket with a pile of books or toys and she will entertain herself for sometimes twenty minutes at a stretch. This is particularly helpful during those moments when I get the urge to shower, brush my teeth, go to the bathroom, make the bed or throw in a load of laundry. Just when I'm getting used to this little luxury, she decides to change the rules without even giving me a heads-up.

I'm in the shower one morning—shaving my legs even!—and having a grand old time of it. I peek out of the shower curtain from time to time, and as usual, she's sitting on the bath mat like a happy little Buddha, self-contained and perfectly content. I condition my hair and exfoliate my elbows and my knees, and when I'm finished, I slide open the curtain to see Sophie on her hands and knees, rocking forward and back like a cat about to pounce on a lizard in the grass.

We've done our requisite hours of tummy time and she's pulled herself up into the all-fours position before, but this is the first time she's made these launching motions.

"Are you getting ready to crawl, baby?" I ask. The sound of my voice startles her and shatters her concentration, and she falls into a prone position, frustrated and angry. She puts her little forehead on the ground, the picture of defeat.

I quickly pat myself dry, grab a robe and whisk her to her bedroom, the only room in the house with carpet. For the next hour she pushes and rocks, her chubby little arms shaking from the effort. I sit three feet from her with her favorite stuffed dog, willing and encouraging her to take that first quadruped step.

"Come and get your doggy!" I urge her, aching with the frustration of not being able to help her make this symbolically quantum leap.

She wants it. Badly. I can see it in her eyes and in her resolve. I crawl around her in circles, trying to show her how it's done.

Showoff, her angry eyes accuse me, so I stop.

She's so close! I want to run and grab the video camera, but I'm afraid if I do, I'll miss the maiden voyage. I also don't want to pick her up and take her with me to fetch it, fearing that when I put her back down, she'll have lost the urge to try altogether. She rocks and I cheer, and then abruptly, one rigid arm shoots forward and lands on the ground ahead of her. She squeals, which makes her lose her balance and fall. Undeterred, she pops right back up like a surfer catching a wave, and all of a sudden it's like I'm watching muscle memory in action. The little arm shoots out again—and the knee behind it automatically follows. The other arm wobbles out, and with it the other knee. Three, four, five times she repeats the sequence before plopping down in a panting heap. She rolls over on her back, giggling and gurgling and altogether delighted with herself.

I, on the other hand, am crying tears of pure joy and relief (because I haven't fully grasped the fact that my brief but blessed windows of freedom are about to slam shut).

From this moment on Sophie is a girl-on-the-go. She crawls every-where, the knees of all of her pants gray with dirt and plastered with dog and cat hair. I consider tying a pair of those magnetic Swiffer pads around her legs, but really that would only be redundant. She doesn't even seem to mind creeping along the unforgiving tile and hardwood that make up the bulk of our home's flooring. The kid is on a mission to move.

Crawling as a singular activity soon loses its novelty and Sophie swiftly graduates to pulling herself up. On everything. Once she's thusly mobile, I start to notice something worrisome: Our house is, in fact, not just a building that happens to house a small family. It's also a complete munitions store of lethal weaponry. Sharp corners jut out at every possible elevation and angle. Toxic chemicals lurk behind easy-to-open doors. Glass and metal and hazardously pointy doodads perch precariously atop shaky tables, and in every room, window nooses—I mean sashes—dangle at dangerously low heights.

"We need to baby-proof the house!" I announce to Joe with alarm the day I make this startling discovery. You'd think that with all of the reading I've done, I might have been at least somewhat prepared for this moment. But until Sophie actually started moving, it didn't feel particularly urgent. Now it seems downright dire.

"We do?" he asks sincerely.

Be patient, I tell myself. *He hasn't read all of the books yet.* I plunge ahead.

"Yes, we do," I snap. "Okay, so here's what I'm thinking." I hand him several dozen pages of Internet printouts featuring security devices that range from window wedges and "cord control kits" to toilet seat locks and table-corner cushions. There's even one for doorknob sleeves that prevent little hands (and often, I suspect, big hands) from oper-ating doors. Joe briefly looks up at me from the pile of papers, then continues to leaf through it.

"A *bumper bonnet?*" he asks incredulously, waving an admittedly ridiculous photo of a child in colorfully padded full-head regalia in front of my face. "You can't be serious."

"Okay, that one I was on the fence about," I admit. "But we definitely need the door and drawer locks. And the corner cushions. And the gates..."

"Did your parents have any of this stuff when you were a kid?" he demands.

"Of course not!" I yelp. "But since when do we hold up *our* parents as models of excellence?"

"Jenna, do you really think all of these things are necessary? Did you ever think maybe having them prevents kids from learning what's safe and what's not?"

"So we're going to let Sophie burn her hand on the stove and drink ammonia so that she can figure out that these are bad ideas?" I'm bordering on hysterical here, but I genuinely cannot believe that Joe is so arrogant—or so lazy—that he doesn't feel the need to create a safe environment for our baby.

"You want to know what I think? I think this stuff is pure marketing crap that preys on every parent's worst fears. Sure, there are tons of things around here that could hurt Sophie, but it's not like we're outside funneling beers while she's inside playing with the fireplace poker. We watch her relentlessly. *You* watch her relentlessly. And we're going to teach her what she can and can't touch. Sure, I think we should move the cleaning supplies to one of the upper cabinets and start keeping the spare razor blades in the garage. But are you planning to leave her alone in the bathroom long enough to take a swan dive into the bowl? And what about when we're out at someone else's house and they don't have a lock on the toilet? Isn't it better that we teach her it's off-limits?"

I have to admit that at least he's thought this through and that his reasoning makes decent sense. I promise to try it "his way" for the next week—no cushions, guards or gates—and see how it goes.

I clear out the large, sturdy drawer in the kitchen that Sophie loves to pull up on and fill it with stacks of Tupperware. I rearrange the cutlery drawers so all of the knives are way in the back where they're difficult for even adults to reach. I move the pointiest and most fragile knickknacks to the highest shelves, but leave the unbreakable—but still untouchable—things within her reach.

"That's not a Sophie toy," I say gently when she reaches for the bowl of antique pool balls on the coffee table or the carved wooden dolphin my dad gave me. "*This* is a Sophie toy," I add, handing her one of her squishy books. It's fascinating to watch how quickly she responds to our new mantra. Sometimes I hold things she wants to inspect and tell her "We look with our eyes, not our hands." As long as I replace the "non-Sophie toy" with something that's allowed, usually she accepts the thwart without protest. And when she does get upset, we simply move the party to another room. It's amazing how easily we can distract her.

When friends come over with their children, sometimes I can tell by their looks and their comments that they think we are lazy and unconcerned parents who couldn't be bothered to bubble-wrap our coffee table. But when we visit other people's homes, I am spared having to ask if I can rearrange their furniture or move all of their belongings to protect my child. "Not a Sophie toy," I point out again and again, and because she knows what this means, she almost always complies.

When I mention Sophie's "training" to my stepmother, she seems dubious. "When my three grandsons come over, I have to put *everything* away," she laments. "They stuff cheese into the DVD player, plug up the toilet with hand towels and last week one of them ripped down my $400 custom drapes to make a fort."

"Well, they're boys," I tell her, trying to make her feel better. But I instantly feel bad about the sweeping gender generalization. After all, my husband is a boy, and he's the smartest person I know.

· ·

trip tip

The "Five Second Rule" and Other Disgusting Parenting Practices You Will Embrace

"Uh-oh," Joe remarks one day just as we are putting Sophie into her car seat. "Do you smell something?"

"Like what?" I reply innocently. This is one deadly situation in which early detection is not rewarded.

"A poop, maybe?" he asks, obviously wishing he hadn't mentioned it. His screwed-up face is bad enough, but what happens next goes far beyond any sense of human decency or comprehension. By the time I realize what is about to transpire, it's a done deal.

"False alarm!" he reports with gusto, inspecting one still-fresh finger.

For a split second I am speechless, an event that occurs as often as I win the lottery.

"Did you just *stick your finger* into her diaper?" I ask incredulously, with no small amount of disgust.

"Yeah," he says nonchalantly. "Why?"

"*Why?*" I stammer. "Because she could have had a poop in there!"

"Yeah, but she didn't," he says proudly. "It's all good."

It actually isn't good at all, but it's life. (My life, at any rate, but probably yours, too, if you're reading this.) Now, one could argue that—assuming there's no changing table or pad nearby—it would not be all that difficult to peek in there and take a visual inventory, but in truth some babies have more rolls than a Charmin factory, which makes it darned near impossible to determine if a particular tyke has or hasn't dropped a bomb. Hence, the employment of what's commonly referred to as the Dipstick Test.

Since parents usually have a stockpile of wet wipes and antibacterial cleansers on hand, and since, in all likelihood, it's not as if our virgin digits have never made contact with dookie, this shouldn't be a scenario that breeds widespread panic and revolt. I'm not saying a person should go out of his or her way to manhandle a baby's waste, but one might want to be prepared for the event—or at least institute a policy on the matter that all parties can enthusiastically support. (For the record, I'd rather cart her back to the house, fumble with the front door lock, haul her to the changing table, remove her shoes and pants and diaper and take my chances that it was all a big, fat waste of time *every stinking time*—pun intended. And as soon as I explain to Joe that he doesn't stand a chance of touching *me* the same week I see him sporting a crap-covered finger, he jumps on board.)

Ironically, it was the Dipstick King who declared early in the game—before Sophie was even born, in fact—that he would claw out his own eyeballs if he ever saw me do the Spittle Swipe on any of our unborn future children. (You know the move: Baby or child has a dried splotch of gunk on her face, and the parent—usually mom—licks her *own* finger to

trip tip

moisten and remove it. I can see by the shuddering that you are familiar with this maneuver.)

"Promise me you won't do it, under *any* circumstances," Joe implored. "Not even if her face is smeared with jelly and there's a swarm of bees circling her head, okay?" Since the man clearly had issues—which resulted in actual nightmares—about this, I had no choice but to promise. (And really, unless we're talking about hiding an advanced case of syphilis or serving up foods that were processed in a plant that also processes peanuts, what he doesn't know won't kill him.)

If you haven't had your baby yet, or s/he is still but a wee blob at this point, I can see how you might insist that your hygiene standards are far too high to permit such behaviors. You may truly believe that pre-chewing another person's food for them is a vile and reprehensible act in which you will never partake, even though you wept when you saw mother Emperors selflessly regurgitating their dinners to nourish their young in *March of the Penguins*. You might feel completely confident that there's nothing in the world that could ever impel you to insert a pastel plastic ball syringe deep into another human being's nasal cavity for the express purpose of sucking out his or her boogers. And I'm positive there's at least one mom-to-be out there who doesn't quite accept that she might one day taste or temperature-test her own breast milk by—you guessed it—taking a nice, hearty swig.

Here's a little newsflash: You will do many, if not all, of these things at least once, but probably on a regular basis. If not, then you will watch your partner do them. Because sometimes, they simply have to be done—even if one parent has to turn a blind eye and pretend it didn't happen.

Fortunately, Joe and I are of like mind when it comes to the Five Second Rule. A stray Cheerio hurdles itself from Sophie's highchair tray? "Five second rule!" we shout in unison, diving for the reckless ring and waving it around for good measure before returning it to its fate. Her bottle slides out of her mouth and onto the carpet mid-feeding? "Five second rule!" we chirp, giving the nipple a cursory swipe with a sleeve and inserting it back into Sophie's mouth. Her pacifier pops out of her mouth and lands under the chair of the people dining at the next table? "Five second rule!" we whisper, trying nonchalantly to retrieve the wayward sucker with our non-pincer grasping feet. When it comes up covered in carpet fuzz and unidentifiable food particles, Joe does what any self-sufficient guy's guy would do in this situation: He dunks it in his beer.

"Alcohol is a sterilizer," he informs me, popping the thing into his own mouth to suck out any remaining malt before giving it back to Sophie.

(Incidentally, in my experience, the Five Second Rule is pretty laid-back as regulations go. I mean, no one is actually *counting* or watching the clock or anything, so sometimes the window of opportunity may get pried open for a significantly longer period. Any reasonable amount of time, particularly if no one but you saw the item go down, is generally acceptable.)

All of that being said, I would be remiss if I didn't add here that some interesting studies actually have looked at the (lack of) wisdom of this practice. Turns out, germs are tenacious little cretins, and it takes approximately one one-hundredth of a nanosecond (or something like that) for one or more malicious microbes to adhere to a fallen object.

trip tip

The more moisture-logged and/or porous the object, and the slicker the surface it lands on, the more bacteria-laden it will become. In other words, drop a syrup-soaked square of French toast onto a cool, smooth tile and five seconds might as well be five years.

On the other hand, exposure to germs helps bolster fledgling immune systems! And if you think about it, it's not like you live in a hermetically sealed bubble. You put your diaper bag on the ground at restaurants, on the floor of filthy subway cars, in the parking lot next to your minivan, and then you come home and jauntily set it on the kitchen table, the one you eat at a dozen or more times a week. Your cat covers his own poop with his paws, the very ones he uses to prance across your pillow each night, the same pillow you bury your face in moments later. You think that sponge that's been festering in your kitchen sink for the past year—the one you "wash" your dishes with before pronouncing them "clean"—is particularly sterile? If someone offered you twenty bucks, would you lick your refrigerator handle or front door knob? And let's not even talk about how long it's been since you replaced your toothbrush. No matter how neat-freakish you'd like to think you are, most of our homes aren't going to win any sanitation awards. And we've made it this far.

The bottom line is that with caution and good sense, giving your child's pacifier the occasional beer bath or cleaning his face with a dab of parental saliva probably won't do him too much harm. Now, make a habit of feeding junior the dust-covered, double-glazed maple scone nuggets you find decaying near the half-price filter display at Starbucks, and you're on your own.

19

Load up the Wagon—
We're Hitting the Road

Before we had a baby, Joe and I loved nothing more than taking off on a spontaneous road trip. Because we were both self-employed, this was fairly easy to pull off. We'd stuff some snacks in a bag, grab a pair of jeans and a sexy nightie (for me! Joe does *not* wear lingerie, okay?) and maybe a nice bottle of wine, and the world was our proverbial oyster. Half the time, we didn't even know where we were going until we got there. If we forgot something, we bought it. Our criteria were simple (bed, running water, toilet paper), our schedule as wide-open as the road.

Boy, how things have changed.

Although most of our immediate family came to visit shortly after Sophie's debut, we've yet to take her to meet her extended network, the great aunts and uncles and second-cousins-twice-removed with whom she shares a sliver of DNA. Since we live in a small town and they live in another small town—four hundred miles away—flying would take twice as long as driving, so we're taking this show on the road.

Foolishly, I start making my packing list on a Post-it note. After both sides are covered in scribbles, I transfer the legible ones to a letter-size notepad. When I run out of room, Joe offers to create an Excel spreadsheet.

"We don't need a *spreadsheet* for a weekend," I tell him.

He raises one eyebrow artfully. I hate it that he can do that and I can't.

"Jenna, let me see that list," he demands.

"See, more than half the things on this list are items we'll bring every time we go away for even one night," Joe explains patiently, highlighting the recurring items that we will be packing regardless of the destination or method of transport. (So far, this list includes bottles, backpack, sippy cups, stroller, changing pad, pacifiers, pac-n-play, travel blanket, tweezers, diapers, wipes, diaper cream, digital camera, digital camera charger, assorted batteries, baby monitor, books, bottled water, nail clippers, noise machine, nightlight, toys, thermometer, Tylenol, Ziploc bags, clothes, socks, snacks, bibs, baby shampoo, sunblock, sling, favorite stuffed dog, first aid kit and one condom—just in case.) Then, he tells me, he'll create a separate column for travel by car, air or boat, and a third column labeled "current trip" for items like hostess, birthday or wedding gifts and tampons. The guy is nothing if not thorough.

Since we're going by car this time—and the car seat is permanently installed so we're not likely to forget it—the "current trip" column is almost empty. This is fortunate, because if it had anything on it bigger than an amoeba, it wouldn't fit in the car.

"Do we really need all of this stuff for a two-day trip?" Joe asks when he sees the pile of stuff towering near the front door on our departure day.

"Do *you* want to be responsible for packing?" I ask snarkily. "You're welcome to go through it all and take out what you think we don't need," I add, knowing yet still praying this won't happen.

"Whatever," Joe says. "We can just leave what we don't need in the car."

"It's not like I have a disco ball and our ski gear in there," I add defensively. This is simply the stuff we use every day. It's astonishing when you think about it, really. When did life get so complicated?

We've made this trip dozens of times and—without a baby—it typically takes us about six and a half hours. Because I know that Joe isn't too keen on stopping every hour for potty and food breaks, I usually try to pack lots of snacks and limit my liquid consumption. We realize early into the trip that this isn't going to be necessary. Our tiny co-captain is calling the shots now (loudly, at times). She needs to eat frequently, and until you've tried spoon-feeding a child who's strapped into a seat directly behind the seat you're strapped into as you hurdle along at 75 mph, you don't know frustrating. Sophie gets bored and fussy looking at any toy for more than four and a half minutes. And no matter what CD we put in, it would appear that she doesn't approve of our musical tastes.

"How far have we gone?" I shout over Sophie's latest fit.

"Thirty-four miles," Joe replies dolefully.

I play peek-a-boo through the opening between my seat and the headrest until my neck begins to throb. I give her water (which she drops), Cheerios (which she spills), a book (which she throws at my head). We try every silly, engaging song we know, but "Pop! Goes the Weasel" makes her wail and "This Old Man" doesn't fare any better.

Starting to feel carsick, I turn and stare at the road ahead. She's up in arms and we are totally helpless.

"This sucks," Joe says.

That about sums it up.

"In the jungle, the mighty jungle, the lion sleeps tonight," I croon absentmindedly, mostly in an effort to drown out Sophie's frustrating whimpering sounds. Amazingly, she stills. She likes it! Joe and I exchange nervous glances. "In the jungle, the mighty jungle, the lion sleeps tonight!" we sing together. Sophie giggles.

"A winga-wa, a winga-wa, a winga-wa, a winga-wa—Near the village, the peaceful village, the lion sleeps tonight..."

If you're not familiar with this tune, it's an old African doo-wop song featuring three simple, repetitive verses peppered with indecipherable Zulu chanting (and my apologies to songwriter Solomon Linda for not knowing how to spell or translate Zulu and subsequently massacring the surely beautiful meaning). Few people know the actual words, but it's a catchy little ditty even when you make up your own lyrics.

An hour flies by in what feels like fourteen, but who's counting? As long as we are chanting, Sophie is enthralled.

"Oh, eeeeeeeeeeeee, e, e, e, e, I'm on my way!" We're really getting into it now. After a few minutes, I chance a backward glance and wouldn't you know it, Sophie's fast asleep. I keep singing and nudge Joe, motioning that he should look.

"Should weeeeeeeeeeeeee, e, e, e, e, a-keep sing-ing?" he croons, wide-eyed and hopeful but not missing a beat.

"Oh yes, we should, oh yes, we should, oh yes, we should..." I answer in tune.

Eight hours, five stops and two hoarse throats later, we arrive at my sister-in-law's house.

"We have to do this again in forty-eight hours," I say miserably when Joe kills the engine.

"We could just move here," he replies. We certainly have enough stuff.

"I'd consider it," I mumble.

"You get Sophie and I'll get the stuff," Joe offers.

That's definitely one deal I'm not going to turn down. I lift her sleepy, sweaty but still sweet-smelling body from the car seat just as the front door of the house swings open and bodies come hurtling at us and crushing us all in giant bear hugs.

"Whoa!" Uncle Steve laughs when he sees our overstuffed SUV. "You guys planning to stay for a while?"

"Thanks, we'd love to," I tell him, handing Sophie to him and hauling the biggest duffle bag up onto my shoulder.

Aunt Juli looks horrified.

"I'm kidding, guys," I assure them. "We're leaving on Sunday."

"And heading on a cross-country trek afterwards?" Juli laughs, stealing Sophie away from Steve's arms.

"Maybe," I tell them, heaving more crap from the car.

The next two days are heaven. Aunts, uncles, cousins and grand-parents fight for the privilege of holding, changing and feeding Sophie. Joe and I have a conversation—uninterrupted—that lasts an entire twelve minutes. Sophie obviously loves all of the attention, and her relatives can't get enough of her. We tack on an extra day, partly because we're having such a great time, and partly to postpone the inevitable return trip.

"I have an idea," I say to Joe as we buckle our squirming baby into her seat. "I saw a Borders right by the on-ramp to the highway."

"Latte or 'The Lion Sleeps Tonight'?" he asks.

"Both," I answer.

We're getting better at this every day.

. . . .

trip tip

Oh, the Places You'll Go: What You Should Know Before Traveling With Baby

IF YOU THINK taking care of a baby is challenging in the comfort and confines of your own home, just wait until the first time you attempt to transfer her from Point A to Point B. Keep this tip sheet handy should you ever decide to be so bold:

- However many diapers you think you might need for your trip, triple it. Carry no fewer than two in your pocket, four in your purse, seven in your snack bag, twenty-two in your carry-on and another three or four hundred in your biggest suitcase. Stick in a Ziploc bag filled with at least a dozen wet wipes alongside every stash. You may accidentally grab the wrong bag when you head into the rest stop/fast-food bathroom/airplane lavatory, and once you've removed the old stinky nappy, you're basically screwed. On the way home from one trip, I discovered—to my horror, after I'd already disposed of the soiled diaper—that my purse stash was completely depleted. I yelled out to Joe to grab me one from the car, but that supply was gone, too. We were miles away from civilization, so we sat on a bench with our bare-bottomed babe until another mom strolled up, at which point we casually asked if she would sell us a diaper. (She generously handed one over, free of charge. Thanks lady, whoever you are!) But really, it's not wise to count on the kindness of strangers. You could get stuck at a nasty rest area for days.

- When you're waiting at the gate to board a plane with your tot, know there's a reason why they offer pre-boarding to families with small children. *Take them up on this.* Until you travel with a baby, you surely cannot imagine how difficult it is to maneuver her squirming body, her FAA-approved car seat, your purse, her shoes (that they made you remove at the security checkpoint—not because she looks particularly menacing, but because they'll be damned if they're going to be accused of profiling—and which she refuses to let you put back on) and all of her in-flight necessities down that ridiculously narrow aisle between the seats. It is not fun or pretty, and I secretly believe that if terrorists knew how easy it is to scalp passengers with the jagged corner of an unwieldy car seat, the apparatuses would be banned from the skies forever.

- When traveling by air, buy the kid her own seat. Yes, it's expensive. And sure, she'd prefer to sit in your lap. But plenty of studies have shown that she's safest strapped into her own seat. Plus, having the extra space allows you the flexibility of moving her once she's driven the businessman in the seat in front of her to the brink of homicide with her relentless kicking/wailing/pretzel tossing. This luxury cannot be overstated.

- When traveling by *any* method of public transport, practice your "I'm *so* sorry" face for several weeks in a mirror until you achieve the perfect balance between conscientious

trip tip

and contrite. You might even consider having small business cards printed with this phrase that you can pass out
to other passengers in advance. You might be shocked
by the number and frequency of dirty looks you will
get when your kid throws a fit (unless you're traveling
in Portugal, where they seem to adore crying babies; the
surlier, the better). A belligerent "I hear her louder than
you do, pal" might be accurate, but does little to endear
you to your temporary neighbors.

- Take a train whenever you can. If there's no train going
  where you're going, go somewhere else! Trains are fun!
  Trains have dining cars! There are fun things to look
  at out the windows! The bathroom is bigger than a
  breadbox—and you can use it whenever you like! You
  can nurse a baby right in your seat! Pass her back and
  forth* between yourself and your partner (and occasionally, another bored and kindly traveler)! Many trains even
  serve adult beverages! Need I say more?

  *DISCLAIMER: I didn't say this was *wise*, I just said
  it was an option. When traveling by any method,
  baby is always best protected when securely fastened
  into an approved safety seat. Just because your dad
  let you ride in a lawn chair in the back of his ancient
  pickup truck when you were a kid doesn't mean this
  was a smart move. You're lucky to be alive, sister.
  But you're an adult now and you can make your
  own choices.

- Everyone tells you to bring a change of clothes for the
  baby. Seeing as babies traditionally have very poor motor
  skills, not to mention little control over their bodily

functions, they tend to get messy. To all but the greenest rookie, the spare onesie is a given. But no one mentions that when baby spills/pukes/suffers a GI blowout, studies (conducted by me, over and over and over) show that she is always sitting on mom's lap. And unless your partner tends to dress in a feminine assortment of layered garments, you'll be glad you stuffed that little slipdress in your bag.

- Forget about how you look. Really. I mean, sure, change out of your puke- and poop-stained clothes when you can, but when traveling with a small child you are going to look like the living dead. Accept this. And who really cares? Have you ever in your life bumped into someone you sat next to on a plane in 1997? No! They go away, you go away and the worst that can happen is that some guy in Topeka occasionally wonders what happened to that frazzled lady who had really bad hair, small chocolate handprints on her boob and something green stuck between her front teeth. As God is my witness, I once read this bit of advice on a "traveling with kids" web site: "Take lipstick and a small mirror in your hand luggage. If you're having a bad time, take two minutes to put on some lipstick and give yourself a pep talk in the mirror." This writer should be arrested and her keyboard should be confiscated. Screw the lipstick. If you have two whole minutes (which you won't), go to the bathroom alone. This might be the last time you get to do this for the next eleven years.

- Barf bags are enormously underrated. Not, of course, for their intended purpose; in that case they're almost useless where a baby is concerned. When she barfs—and she

trip tip

will—the odds that you will have time to retrieve, open and position the thing properly in order to catch the fallout are 1 in 564,983,203 (actual figure). But since they are complimentary, grab every one within reach. They work great for carrying poopy diapers until you can locate an inconspicuous trash bin, come in handy for stashing the messy remains of half-eaten bananas and semi-chewed prunes, can be fashioned into a mouthpiece to help relieve hiccups, and if you're creative and have a crayon or two floating around in your bag, you've got an instant hand puppet. (Please note: Do not attempt any of the above if the barf bag actually has barf in it.)

- It's one of the basic laws of the universe: Travel rules are different from home rules. Like, for instance, at home you might not consider a king-size bag of Doritos and a Diet Dr Pepper "dinner." But in the car? Bon appétit! Likewise, although you may abhor televised entertainment and refuse to succumb to the lure of Nickelodeon's "free babysitting" service at home, if back-to-back viewings of your host's Dora the Explorer video is keeping junior happy, I suggest turning a blind eye. Studies (see above) prove that this will not, as you might fear, irreparably harm your child. And you might even get a fifteen-minute nap out of the deal.

- Consider other passengers—carefully—when packing. This means loading your carry-on with lots of studious but engaging books, stickers and puzzles—and leaving the annoyingly cheerful Wiggle Giggle Gorilla at home. Years ago a friend told me about a flight she was on where a couple traveling with a small baby handed out earplugs to every passenger on the plane. I made a mental note that very day, and I have shamelessly stolen this move now a dozen or more times. I am here to tell you, the response is overwhelming! Grumpy and gratefully, temporarily deaf old men will actually go out of their way to lean over you to coochie-coochie-coo your child's chin. Flight attendants will offer you complimentary headsets. Strangers of all ages will smile and wave as you pass them (again and again) on your way to the loo. Best twenty bucks you'll ever spend.

trip tip

20

....

School Daze:
Did I Miss the Memo?

At a mere ten months old, Sophie's bag of tricks is overflowing: She sits, stands, crawls and claps her hands. She waves goodbye. Drinks from a cup. Recognizes herself in a mirror. Understands simple commands. Says "Mama" and "Dada" (and frequently, "Bobby," despite the fact that we can't think of a soul we know who goes by this name or anything resembling it).

Soon enough, she's contemplating the mother of all milestones: The First Steps.

Remember back when you first told people you were pregnant and they'd say ominously, "Your life is never going to be the same"? And do you remember how hard it was to bite your tongue and *not* say, "Really? Jeez! I thought I was going to get to keep on eating bonbons and bungee jumping and living the life of luxury and leisure all day, every day!" Well, when these same folks notice your toddler tottering on the brink of mobility, they'll resume the dire yet obvious predictions with startling enthusiasm: "Well, lookey there. She's about to walk! *Your life is never going to be the same,*" these geniuses will comment sagely.

The thinly veiled doomsday prophecy often is accompanied by an annoying clucking of the tongue, which, as far as I can discern, is just for bad measure.

I'm here to tell you they're right: Life *does* change when your toddler actually starts toddling—for the better. Within a day of Sophie's maiden upright voyage, my OxiClean consumption is reduced by half, and the persistent ache in my back begins to subside. That's it. Life isn't harder by any means; in fact, for me it becomes much, much simpler. When Sophie gets tired of sitting in her stroller, I don't have to carry her, because she can walk! (Sure, my tiny pedestrian has her own ideas about destinations, but we find ways to work around this.) Her pants no longer sport matching grubby knees. Since she already knows for the most part what she can and can't touch, the need to keep her curiosity in check neither decreases nor increases. Sophie isn't just happier and cleaner, but she's *way* easier to pick up when she's vertical than she was when she was horizontal. I think I am in heaven.

Sophie isn't just walking the walk; she's really starting to talk the talk. Monosyllabic grunts give way to complex, compound declarations like "want ball" and "doggy woof." If someone gave us a nickel for every time Joe and I looked at each other, shook our heads and declared our daughter a genius, I'd be too busy cruising the Greek isles to finish writing this book.

"Is Sophie registered for preschool yet?" asks a frighteningly well-dressed mom I meet at the park. We've been pushing our daughters on neighboring swings for at least a half an hour. Three-year-old Priscilla, I have been told, attends the impossibly posh preschool just up the road from Oprah's $50-million pad. Even if there weren't a waiting list three miles long to get into Le Petit Billionaire (not the actual name), I can't see us forking over five figures for two half-days of upmarket daycare any time in the foreseeable future.

"Uh, no," I tell Ms. Moneybags (which may or may not be her real name; I was too stupefied to ask). "I know Sophie seems mature because she's so bright," I add, "but she's not even a year old yet."

"Prissy was enrolled before she was conceived!" Moneybags trills. "*Obviously* it's too late for Le Petit, but maybe there's somewhere else…" Her voice drifts off, *obviously* implying that I am hopelessly screwed.

Sometimes when I see really old people, my first involuntary thought is *Boy, I'm sure glad I'm not old*. As if they got the short stick in the age-group lottery while—lucky me!—I get to be relatively young and agile. It seems impossible to grasp the fact that the balding, freckled old broad over there used to be a babe, and that she's just farther along in the process than I am, but (God willing and if I'm really lucky), I'll get there, too. Likewise, this is how I've always felt when the inevitable preschool conversation comes up: Not my concern. See, I've just got a *baby*. And babies don't *go* to preschool, so you can just sell your preschool elsewhere.

But now I start thinking about it. And researching it. I find study after study proving preschool offers a lifetime of benefits not just for the child but for society as a whole. (Apparently someone's even found a link between preschool and government spending on crime reduction and social services.)

"Sophie doesn't need to go to preschool," Joe says definitively when I bring up the idea. "We didn't go to preschool," he adds, performing an exaggerated ticking motion with his head, "and we turned out okay."

"Funny," I say, my tone implying I think otherwise, "but she *does* need to go to preschool. Not now, but when she's two or three. Now that I'm working part-time again, she'd be with a babysitter anyhow. She might as well be learning something when she's not with us. Plus, she is going to need the socialization and the stimulation."

"Socialization and stimulation?" Joe asks suspiciously. "Who have you been talking to?"

"Look, honey, Sophie is going to need to be around other kids, so she can learn to share and wait and take turns and all that stuff," I explain. "As far as stimulation goes, we both know I'm not good at coming up with a new game every hour. We've sorted all of the dry beans into the egg carton a thousand times and we pick up all five hundred cotton balls with the tongs at least once a day. Frankly I'm getting pretty low on creative ideas here. In another year, I'll be completely out. Preschool teachers take classes and read books on how to keep kids entertained while they're learning. You really can't put a price on that."

"How much does it cost?" he asks with alarm.

"Depends on if we can even get *in* anywhere," I remind him, trying my best to sound ominous. "I'll let you know when I figure it out."

With the help of some experienced friends, I fill out a dozen college-length applications, find a family photo that doesn't have any beer bottles or wine glasses in the background, make copies of it and send the packets off.

I get zero replies. I start to get a little panicky when it occurs to me that we may have to register for a home-schooling license.

One day I'm taking Sophie for a walk in our neighborhood when I notice a tiny "Preschool" sign on a side door of a church. Since I can see this church from my front door, it's astonishing to me that I've never noticed the sign before. We march up and knock on the director's door, where we are told there are two spots left for the following fall.

"Does she have to be potty trained?" I ask. How can I possibly know whether or not she'll be potty trained in sixteen months?

"Nope," the director says, shaking her head.

"And the teacher?" I ask hopefully.

"She's amazing," the director says. "Been doing this twenty-seven years. Has won more awards than any other preschool teacher in town. You can go next door and meet her if you'd like."

"And how much is the tuition for two days a week?" *Please say less than the cost of a new Mercedes.*

She rattles off a number that doesn't seem appallingly high; I quickly calculate that in the end it will be *less* than what we pay for babysitting at home.

"Who do I make the check out to?" I ask, fishing my checkbook out of the bag in the stroller.

That night, I tell Joe that Sophie is enrolled in preschool. We both look at our tiny, helpless child and agree that it is impossible to picture her going off to school. I must look as overwhelmed as I feel by this idea, because Joe gives my hand a squeeze.

"It's not for another year and a half," he reminds me. Still. School? People say they grow up fast, but this is ridiculous.

21

The Definition of Insanity

From almost the moment Sophie was born, armies of annoyingly nosy people have been asking us if we plan to have more babies. The minute we say "yes" or "probably" or even "that's the eventual plan," they demand to know the tentative due date. Before we can answer, they proceed to tell us precisely why the way they spaced out their own children is the only way to do it—as if this is something we could control with any degree of predictability anyhow.

Of course, I can't tell them the real answer, which is the combined, as-yet-unknown date in the probably not-too-distant future after which a) I can fit back into my old pre-pregnancy jeans, and b) I can stomach the thought of giving up my beloved but possibly listeria-contaminated deli turkey, feeling like constant crap and wearing my wardrobe of tent dresses again.

"How could we possibly love another child as much as we love Sophie?" I ask Joe one night. I am genuinely concerned about this.

"Could we think another baby was as beautiful or as smart?" he adds.

We sit in silence.

"My mom always said she loved all of her children differently but equally," I offer.

"Did you believe her?" Joe asks.

"No," I tell him.

More silence.

"Wait!" he says, inspiration striking. "I love my sisters differently but equally. You love *your* brother and sister differently but equally."

"You're right!" I answer. "And we love Max and Sam differently but equally!"

This is not exactly true. Sam is his dog; Max is my cat. Suffice it to say if the house were on fire, the animal that got saved first would depend on which one of us was crazy enough to run back in.

He ignores my joke. "So it's possible," he says.

We leave it at that for now.

Sophie's first birthday comes and goes. With it we make a startling discovery: Between her birthday and the year's smattering of holidays, we may never need to buy her anything—except food—for any reason whatsoever for the rest of her life. Friends and relatives shower her with more clothes, books, toys, shoes, picture frames and hair accessories (despite an obvious lack of hair) than any one person has business owning.

To make room for all of the new stuff, I gather up all of the clothes she's outgrown and sort them into nesting boxes in the garage. The boxes are labeled "girl clothes, 0-3 mos," "girl clothes, 3-6 mos" and so on. Every time I haul a load out there, I wonder if I'll ever use these things again. It's such an awesome thought: I could create another person…or ten…or none.

"You'd better have another baby before all of this stuff goes out of style," jokes my sister one day, eyeing the twin towers of baby and maternity clothes.

"You'd better have another baby before Sophie gets too accustomed to having everything—you, her toys, her room—all to herself," adds my sister-in-law on the phone one evening.

"You'd better have another baby before it gets too easy with Sophie and you decide you don't have the energy to start over," insists my stepmom, a mother of eight, every time we chat.

"If you're going to have another baby, you should know the risk of complications goes up every year after you turn thirty-five," declares my OB at my annual exam.

I just turned thirty-four. I've got eleven months. In the scheme of things, not a whole lot of time.

Mulling this information over, I go to my closet and swing open the door. I reach in and retrieve a cute little slipdress, a recent purchase. I step out of my sweats and shimmy into the dress. I turn sideways and place my hand on my stomach. It's still a little soft and squishy, but (in clothes, at least) it doesn't look all that different than it did before I had Sophie. I glance at my perfect, beautiful baby playing quietly in the next room, and for the four hundredth time, marvel at the fact that she was made in my body. She lived in there—and she came out of *there*. And she's not a baby anymore.

I step out of the dress, hang it carefully back on its hanger and place it back into the closet. Then I walk into the bathroom, open the medicine cabinet and remove my birth control pills.

"Here we go again," I say with a bravado I don't quite feel, tossing them into the trash.

· ·

Epilogue

[*Interior:* DOCTOR'S *office, six months later. A visibly pregnant* JENNA *sits on a doctor's examination table.* JOE *sits on the chair next to her, holding her hand. They exchange nervous glances. The* DOCTOR *enters the room.*]

DOCTOR Hey, you guys, nice to see you! [*Gives* JOE *a man-smack on the back*] You ready to do this deal? [*laughs*]

JENNA Ready as we'll ever be.

DOCTOR We going to find out the sex today?

JENNA We sure hope so.

DOCTOR Think you know what it is this time?

JENNA No idea. But this pregnancy is totally different than the last one. I'm craving vegetables all the time. Maybe it's a boy. [*Glances at* JOE]

[*The* DOCTOR *nods noncommittally, switches on a machine, squirts some gel onto* JENNA'S *belly. He retrieves the machine's wand, presses it to her swelling stomach and begins moving it around.*]

DOCTOR Man, you two make beautiful babies. Just beautiful. See that
heartbeat? That's what I like to see.

JENNA Anything else?

DOCTOR Picture-perfect vertebrae, nice abdominal wall…let's see,
one, two, three…ten fingers! [*chuckles*]

[JENNA *leans forward to peer at the monitor more closely.*]

JENNA [*annoyed*] Is there a penis or not?!

JOE *Jenna!*

[JENNA *gives* JOE *a "don't you dare give me a dirty look" dirty look.*]

JENNA Well? What is it?

[*The* DOCTOR *looks from* JENNA *to* JOE *and back at the screen. His smile gives
nothing away. Finally, he speaks.*]

DOCTOR [*his voice completely neutral*] It's another girl.

[JENNA *turns her head away from* JOE. *A tear begins to stream slowly down
her face. Damn it, she thinks, wondering what ever happened to the one-boy,
one-girl, nice, neat all-American nuclear family. All of her friends had broth-
ers when she was little, but now it seems like her parent-friends have either all
boys or all girls. Rarely both. And even though—again—she is secretly excited
because she actually wanted Sophie to have a sister, she also feels horribly guilty.*
JENNA *turns when she hears the doctor slip out of the room. She looks at* JOE.
He has a huge, dopey grin on his face.]

JENNA [*suspiciously, wiping at her tears*] Why are you smiling like that?
Aren't you disappointed? You wanted a boy. You *know* you wanted
a boy.

JOE   Jenna, I wanted a boy last time because I thought that was what I was supposed to want. I didn't know any better. This time I know how amazing it is to have a daughter. How could I possibly be disappointed?

JENNA   [*sniffles*] Really?

JOE   Are you kidding me? Of *course*, really.

JENNA   [*laughing*] Are you just trying to get lucky later?

JOE   [*laughing*] That wasn't the goal…but does this mean I might?

[*Camera pans in on* JENNA, *who smiles and winks suggestively. We see* JOE *wrap his arm around her shoulders, open the exam room door and lead her down the hall.*]

Also from Jenna McCarthy:

Cheers to the New Mom/Cheers to the New Dad

(Sasquatch Books, December 2008)

*A clever, flip-cover book
filled with wit and wisdom
for the expectant mom. . .
and the guy who knocked her up.*

Look for it at www.jennamccarthy.com